Another Day, Another Dog

Trevor Rowe

Visit us online at www.authorsonline.co.uk

An Authors OnLine Book

ISBN 0-7552-0263-5

Authors OnLine Ltd
19 The Cinques
Gamlingay, Sandy
Bedfordshire SG19 3NU
England

This book is also available in e-book format, details of which are available at www.authorsonline.co.uk

In memory of my sister,

"Raine"

(1948 – 2005)

and with thanks to

my wife, **Sue,**

without whose patience and help,
particularly in the memory department,
this book would never have been written.

Also dedicated to:

"Hedgehog" Archie
Grand old Arnie
Good old Ben
Raine's Emma and Toby
Little Fergie
My Jason
"Fearsome" Olly
Pagan the Wanderer
Sue's Sebbie
All the Spaniels
Et al,
without whom there would have been no book.

Trevor Rowe

Trevor was born in Kent, England, and has travelled extensively both with his father who had a long career in the British Army and, subsequently, during Trevor's 34 year career in the Royal Air Force.

He "retired" as a Wing Commander in 1993 and after a two year spell with BAe in Saudi Arabia, between long visits to the USA, quite by accident he and Sue fell into house-sitting one summer.

Trevor's interests include golf, the guitar and singing, and his (beloved—Sue says) computers!

He and Sue live adjacent to the Stray in the beautiful spa town of Harrogate on the edge of the Yorkshire Dales.

Table of Contents

Introduction

We fell into house sitting almost by chance and had enjoyed this "retirement" pastime for around four years when I decided during one long stay to jot down a few thoughts in the form of a diary. The main reason for this was to update the owners on all that had happened to their pets and lovely garden during their absence.

They were delighted with my efforts. So many funny and interesting incidents happened in that time and during subsequent periods of residence in other peoples' homes that I decided a more permanent record was deserved and so turned my diaries and other memories into a book.

The early chapters tell how my wife, Sue, and I enjoyed the company of our own animals and of the exotic places we lived, sharing with the reader many of our humorous and some sad experiences over the years.

For example, I'm chastised in a phone call from France because I would not go out in the dead of night to teach our newly acquired bald, inexperienced ex-battery hens to roost. Our pets get into trouble and like all long-term pet owners we suffer a few sad losses along the way.

Our newly married life in North Devon, England, was blissful but was cut short by an unexpected, but most welcome, move to St Louis, Missouri, in the USA and the next portion of the book features our animal encounters in that "great" country.

Returning after three years in America we then spent a year or so in England before another unplanned overseas trip. Our extended stay in Saudi Arabia and our contact there with animals features next, prior to the real subject matter - our house sitting experiences.

We travelled from Northumberland to East Sussex in the course of our "work" and we learned much about some of the villages and their history on the way. There was nothing quite like the peace and tranquillity of a beautiful summer's afternoon in a delightful English country garden. Conversely, lambing during a powerful thunderstorm on a bitterly cold winter's night in February was quite the opposite, particularly when Sue was only supposed to be taking care of the dogs and cats and I was miles away in another house which was struck by lightning.

Five weeks with Olly, the rottweiler, was interesting, challenging but also very enjoyable.

The North Yorkshire Moors, rugged, beautiful and peaceful in summer. But in winter?

And then there was Ben, the elderly cancer stricken Labrador that we had twice to take to the faith healer....

Did I mention the cat up Sue's nose?

No?

Well, please read on....

Chapter One

How It All Began

Her jaws only inches from my face, the Rottweiler uttered a low, menacing growl. I could feel her hot breath on my cheek and her big brown eyes glared, unwavering, into mine. Unable to move, I was pinned down by her weight and I could feel the power behind those jaws, her teeth and her huge shoulders.

I was alone in the house, my mobile phone was out of reach and there was no one within miles. This was her territory and I was an unwelcome intruder. I was terrified!

But hold on a minute, I'm getting ahead of myself. This all happened much later on. I'd better start at the beginning.

We had always had dogs. When my wife Sue and I met, I had a fully-grown Labrador called Jason and she had Sebastian. He was called Sebbie, for short, and he was a real farmyard poodle. By that I mean he was always scruffy and loved the outdoors; not the stereotyped manicured and well groomed lap dog. The Labrador and the poodle became the best of friends and we all lived in or near Harrogate, close to the beautiful North Yorkshire Dales in, arguably, one of the most scenic parts of England.

Eventually, as our dogs enjoyed each other's company so much, and so did we, Sue and I decided that this was it and we should get together permanently. It didn't take us too long to take it a step further and we set up home together with our dogs, not to mention the cat.

This was to be the beginning of a long and satisfying period of our lives, involving ourselves, our extended family and a host of various animals.

To start, Jason had been with me since he was nine weeks old and had been my friend and companion through an earlier unpleasant (aren't they all?), albeit fairly tolerable, separation and divorce. You know, I took the dog and my clothes and she took everything else!

No, that's not true. In case my former wife reads this, we did split everything amicably and had no legal arguments about who took what and maintenance etc. In fact, it was one of the most friendly divorces I have known of and all concerned were, and have been, on good terms ever since. My ex was even good enough to stop her lawyer from pursuing the "screw him for everything you can get" routine for which I am eternally grateful! And she did let me take the dog.

I well remember the joys of Jason as a puppy in addition to the many trials and tribulations along the way. Like all young Labradors he soon became an expert at chewing everything in sight and many other things that weren't. Nothing was sacred and in his time he demolished several pairs of shoes, the whole of one side of a wooden door frame within his reach, together with most of the plaster beside it and one of the cross pieces under a dining table.

However, there is no other puppy as lovable, happy and boisterous as a Labrador and he was a constant source of pleasure and enjoyment and a great playmate for my daughter who grew up with him. Jason and I parted company with the rest of our family when he was around ten years old, two years before I met Sue.

Jason was twelve and a half years old when he suffered his first stroke, having gradually lost most of the use of his back legs over the preceding months. He went downhill all too rapidly and some weeks later I took poor old Jason for his final trip to the vet, leaving tearfully shortly afterwards, carrying only his lead and collar.

Those who have enjoyed the companionship of a trusty dog for any length of time and have suddenly lost such a good friend will know exactly how I felt. I would still hear him in my flat and step with care over the spot in the doorway between the sitting room and kitchen, where he always used to lie. Of course he wasn't there, so there was no need to avoid stepping on him. But old habits die hard, as do old friends.

He was no longer at my side looking up with those big, hopeful, eyes when I prepared a meal, a sandwich or opened the biscuit tin on making a cup of tea. It took several gin and tonics each night to get me through the first few days without him.

I still recall good old Jason with great affection each time I pass the little wooded park, where he took his final walk, opposite the vet's surgery, from which he never emerged.

Now Sue's Sebbie was a very different dog. He was definitely not the kind of poodle that was manicured and coddled, more the type that rolled in horse sh.., liked being covered in mud and pretended to be a much bigger, more aggressive dog. In fact, he always thought he was a spaniel. At least Sue's mother went out to buy her a spaniel all those years ago and came back with a poodle, which might explain a lot about Sebbie's character. He had been a spaniel in his own mind ever since. He was never clipped, poodle fashion, and barely tolerated the occasional haircut now and again.

Sue and I both worked and after two years my job moved from North Yorkshire to Devon way down in the south west of England so we set about planning a weekend to look for a house and a more permanent relationship for us and the animals. We drew a circle on the map within a comfortable commuting distance from my new work place and wrote to various estate agents for details of properties in our chosen area and within our price range. As a good deal of the circle was in the sea our search area was fortunately much reduced!

We also obtained copious copies of the local papers. This was, of course, in the pre-internet era. Will that ever rate as famously as the abbreviations for Before Christ, or Anno Domini I wonder? No, I can't see PI making the history books, can you? I suppose Pre Internet Era might be more memorable but maybe a little overcooked, as most of the dot com companies and other tech stocks on the world markets seemed to be from their inception.

Anyway, armed with a detailed schedule, and the dogs, we set out for pastures new on our two-day house hunting expedition to view properties throughout the weekend.

On our first morning we had looked at many, some good, some bad. We stopped to check our list just after coming out of a pretty little house called Apple Tree Cottage. After a short while a voice from nowhere said, in a broad Devon accent.

"Can I 'elp you m'dears?"

From over the adjacent hedge a head suddenly appeared, followed more sedately by the rest of a white-haired gentleman of some years who looked glad of a respite from mowing his lawn.

"No, thank you very much," we said. "We are just looking for a house to buy and are checking our next stop."

He asked whether we knew that there was a cottage for sale not far down the road. It wasn't on our list but it sounded as though it had potential so we decided to check it out. Despite his comprehensive directions we had considerable trouble finding the place. Eventually, after driving up an impossibly steep hill, twice round a small village green, up the side of a farmhouse, through a cobbled farmyard and up a narrow track, we came across a small cottage nestling in the side of the hill looking badly as though it needed new owners.

The sun shone on the rustic five-barred gate highlighting a carving of two elderly people. At the end of the path leading up to the cottage a beautifully carved wooden swallow perched cheekily on the side of a rose covered porch.

We said to ourselves that we might as well look at the cottage now we were here so we opened the gate and walked up to the old oak front door. A small cartwheel leant nonchalantly against the whitewashed front wall of the cottage as though it had rested there for a hundred years.

Surrounding the old, moss covered, slate-roofed building was a typical country cottage garden, delightfully untidy and with a colourful cornucopia of plants sprouting everywhere. Flowers and shrubs of all kinds intermingled with small lawns and a tiny pond. Away to the south the property looked over a combe and up the other side towards the Taw estuary. A rustic bird table leaning at an impossible angle completed the picture.

At our knock, a lady opened the door and we explained with some apology that we had heard the house was for sale and did she mind if we had a look around. She asked us in and we both stood in silence taking in the character and homeliness of the huge sitting room. It must have been at least thirty feet long and at least half as wide. At one end there was a "walk-in" fireplace complete with a huge, open log fire burning and a traditional bread oven. At the other, there was a smaller fireplace. It had obviously been at least two rooms knocked into one somewhere along the line in its history. The walls were two feet thick, the ceilings impossibly low and old beams were everywhere.

Later Sue and I both agreed that we had made the decision to buy the place as soon as we had entered the cottage. This despite the clutter, (there were boxes and bits and pieces piled to the ceilings everywhere) and the imminent need for renovation. We continued our tour of inspection humming and hahing (how **do** you spell that?) about the condition of this and the state of that, whilst assessing its potential, and left saying we'd let the owner know of our decision. Once in the car we decided that we had better keep to our schedule. However, we both knew that we wanted that cottage as soon as we had walked in and we were only going through the motions in looking at the rest of the properties on our list.

We were looking forward to viewing a "Pixie Cottage" in Dingle Dell. Yes, really! But we were disappointed to find that it was a modern two-up, two-down in a terrace on an overcrowded estate. However, as we had stopped outside, were half out of the car and the curtains were moving, we felt that we had better look as though we were interested and take a look at the place anyway. Why do we always feel embarrassed in such situations? It would have been easy to drive off but, no, we felt that we should give the occupants a chance to sell their neat little home. We were probably the only potential buyers they'd had all day!

The owners were kind to us, showing us round with great pride and offered us bed and breakfast at a reasonable price. We stayed the night and although we were non-committal, they must have thought that we were keen on buying as they offered to discount the purchase price by the B&B charge if we purchased the house. Even with this almost unbelievable offer, the thought never even entered our heads!

Early the next morning, we telephoned the owner of the cottage we had stumbled upon the day before, made an offer, which she accepted and we set off back for Yorkshire hoping that nothing would stand in the way of our purchase. Six weeks later the cottage was ours.

We were only later to find out a possible reason why we had fallen in love with that cottage at first sight and why, subsequently, we felt so peaceful living there. Either by design or pure coincidence, its name was Leys Cottage. We thought nothing much about the name at the time of purchase and wondered who Mr, or Mrs, Ley might have been but were intrigued later to hear about Ley Lines and the myth surrounding them.

Apparently, it all began with a man by the name of Alfred Watkins who, at the age of sixty five when riding across the Herefordshire hills just after World War One, saw a vision of the countryside crossed by glowing wires. He is reported to have said that they linked up all kinds of churches, ancient monuments and other religious or historic sites.

Now, allegedly, Mr Watkins had a more than average partiality for the products of the brewing industry. However, his supporters claimed, and still do, that this had nothing to do with his theory that such buildings or sites were linked together by a series of straight lines. Supposedly, this latticework identified lines of harmony, peace and serenity across the country.

However, there appears to be no factual evidence of the existence of such lines. Many historians dispel the theory as pure bunkum and simply the desire of a few misinformed people wishing to make money by writing books about Alfred Watkins' vision, including Watkins himself.

Whatever the truth may be, there certainly was something special about the atmosphere in our cottage and its location, supposedly on one of these Ley Lines, and we were happy to leave the name as it was during the time we had the pleasure of ownership and residence.

We left Yorkshire for the big move to Devon in a raging snowstorm wondering whether our furniture would make the trip in the removal van lumbering its way slowly southwards behind us. We left it far behind and so had to sleep the first night on the carpet in front of the big log fire, furniture-less in our "new" home. No matter. We were young or, at least, younger then and it was all a great adventure. The carpet was luxuriously thick and the fire glowed through the night. Sebbie thought it was great fun to have us sleep downstairs and he did his best to snuggle up and help keep us warm.

By the time the van reached us the next day it had started snowing again and it was no easy task to get the furniture from the van to the cottage as our lane was so narrow that the van could get no closer than fifty yards from our door. Helping the removal men shift freezer, washing machine, dryer and other such necessities up a slope through slush and mud was not our idea of fun.

Nowadays, when we drive down lanes in Devon and Cornwall, or perhaps the Yorkshire Dales, we do appreciate the problems experienced by furniture removers and drivers of other large trucks

The snow settled and our cottage was cold by the second day after our arrival. We had been used to central heating in Yorkshire but the cottage was without such luxury, having only the two open fireplaces in the sitting room and a solid fuel Rayburn cooker in the kitchen. At least the Rayburn was always fired up and it was very efficient. It also provided a copious supply of hot water and heated a large towel rail in the bathroom.

I had reported to my new office, but Sue, fortunately, although her job had transferred with her, had the luxury of a few days off.

However, some extensive decorating was a necessity and Sue had started the daunting task, wearing her ski suit, warm boots and earmuffs. About halfway through the morning, in the stillness that only a calm, snow-laden countryside can produce, there was a knock at the door. Feeling foolish in her ski wear, Sue answered the door. Our new neighbours stood outside to welcome her with the question, "Would you like to come sledging with us?"

Well, what would you rather do?

"Hurray," Sue said, and promptly downed the paintbrush. She was already dressed for it and off they all went. This was to be the start of a long, and still existing friendship, as we visit the family as often as we can if we are down in their neck of the woods.

Our beautiful cottage was situated about 10 miles north of Barnstaple in the hamlet of Churchill. Life was so good, both for us and Sebbie, that we acquired a fat, "free to a good home" spaniel named Fisky and the two of them would take us for regular walks in the rolling fields and on the beautiful beaches both winter and summer.

He had probably been placed on the "transfer list" as he was completely uncontrollable when he came to us, maybe because we believe he had been left alone all day in his former life. However, with Sebbie as permanent company he soon settled down and with, presumably, less food than in his previous life and certainly lots of exercise Fisky soon became a slim, and most obedient, spaniel.

The views on our frequent dog walks were superb. Rugged cliffs fell away into the sea and the unspoiled countryside stretched eastward to the wild, but impressive terrain of Exmoor. North Devon certainly has some beautiful scenery

I often thought how much Jason would have enjoyed being there and I was not to know that very soon we would acquire a replacement under unusual circumstances in the shape of Spey, a fully-grown Labrador who would come unexpectedly into our lives.

Spey, an unusual name for a male Labrador but here's how it came about. Sue and I used to go skiing quite a bit in the Cairngorm Mountains near Aviemore in Scotland. In fact, a few years before, Sue had worked on the ski slopes up there for a short time and knew several of the local people. We were visiting a friend of hers once and were in the local pub when a seemingly arthritic old Labrador hobbled in. We petted the dog and asked his foreign looking owner how old it was.

" 'E is not old," he said, "I 'ave 'it 'im wiz ze stick becos 'e chase ze sheep." We were shocked and angered by this seemingly guiltless confession and a little later spoke to the pub proprietor, who also happened to be a friend of Sue's.

"If the owner ever goes back home or the dog is taken away from him, please let us know," we said. "We will have him." We left, wishing we could have taken the dog away with us right then.

9

Some weeks later Sue was back at home in Devon and I was away on a business trip to London. Sue received a phone call from our Scottish pub landlord friend. He advised her that the Labrador's French owner, who had been a chef in a local hotel, had left the country and the dog was in the temporary care of a kitchen hand working in the same hotel. The dog was ours if we still wanted him.

Sue immediately telephoned me in London, thankfully pulling me out of a boring meeting. She explained the situation, and that night I drove straight up to Scotland. The next day I sought out the dog and eventually found him living in a decrepit old shack in the woods. The place was filthy. I wondered about the state of hygiene in the hotel kitchen but fortunately never had to put it to the test.

The dog wagged his tail with delight at my approach. He was in much better shape than when I had first seen him and looked years younger. He was obviously well fed on kitchen scraps but his personal hygiene left much to be desired! Still, that wasn't his fault. I threw away his blanket, picked up his bowl and lead and left the shack. Without a second glance at his temporary home, he jumped into the back of my car and we drove straight down to Devon. The dog never looked back and from then on it was as though he had belonged to us all his life.

His French owner had named him after the well-known Scottish River Spey as he had been born and raised on its banks. It seemed an apt name, so we kept it. However, it did cause some interest later on. Many people thought it was Spade, or Speyed, and we had to tell his story countless times.

All three dogs loved the open fields and lived in harmony with the chickens, ducks, sheep, cows, our neighbours and us. Spey, with a little training, happily lost his desire to chase sheep. He loved the sea and would frolic (if that is the right word for a large dog) dangerously in the pebble-filled surf at Heddon's Mouth while Sebbie the poodle would bark encouragement from the cobbly beach.

I would surf off the beach at Saunton Sands and it was difficult to keep Spey on the shore while I rode the waves. Spey would battle his way out through the surf with me and he could never understand how I could ride back on the board faster than he could make it back to the beach. Although Sebbie never liked the water, long sandy beaches were his favourite for walks. He would run even faster than Spey across the flat wet sand and bark furiously at the waves. His puzzled look as he went base over apex into a water-filled wave runnel in the sand, still makes us smile when we recall that moment.

Spey & Sebbie

On the cliff tops he would run unseen under the bracken whilst Spey would bound along appearing above the foliage every now and again like a hippopotamus surfacing for air.

On one crisp and clear winter's morning we were out with our dogs when we came across the local hunt on our tiny village green. They had stopped to gather the hounds and there must have been twenty to thirty dogs milling around getting in the way of the horses and their immaculately clad riders.

Now, whether or not you agree with fox hunting in principle you surely cannot deny that a pack of hounds with horses and riders is part of our English country life heritage. I know that the hunt has been denigrated and often dubbed as the "unspeakable chasing the uneatable" but a hunt in full cry, or even at rest before the chase, does present a magnificent picture.

We had Spey and the spaniel on their leads but Sebbie, being the socialite that he was, insisted on talking to every hound in the pack and we could not catch him in the melee. Before too long the hunt master called for the hunt to move on and they all set off up the lane to continue the quest for their quarry. Sue was trying to get into the pack to rescue Sebbie but he thought that this was his opportunity for more fun and trotted off with the hounds before we could stop him. The whipper-in had seen Sebbie go and told us not to worry, they would only be twenty minutes and that he would bring him back when the hunt was over! Apparently their horseboxes were not too far away and they were almost at the end of their day's outing. Sure enough, a little while later Sebbie trotted back with the pack as a fully-fledged honorary foxhound. He was covered in mud and exhausted but he'd had a great time.

You might have gathered that Sebbie really liked other animals and, in turn, they generally liked him. Cows were among his favourites. We just could not keep him away from them on our walks. Many's the time he would be surrounded by these great beasts and they would lick him until he was soaking wet. He had absolutely no fear of them despite the huge difference in size. On other occasions he would unwittingly pretend to be a lamb and did a passably good imitation. He was lamb-sized and roughly the same shape and was often mistaken by the ewes for one of their own. It would only be when they were close enough to catch his scent that the sheep would realise their mistake and there'd be much stamping of forelegs and Sebbie would be firmly pushed away by over-protective mothers.

Of all the houses we have either owned, or in which we have lived, perhaps Leys Cottage is the one we remember with most affection. Peacefully nestling on a hillside off the beaten track yet it was not too far from my office, the nearest town of Barnstaple, and numerous beautiful beaches. It was the sort of place one could leave unlocked with no fear of intrusion at night or even if away for the weekend. We would wake up on summer mornings; the windows wide open and revel in the sounds of the countryside and adjacent farm noises. No alarm clocks needed when there are cows nearby to be milked!

I said peacefully nestling off the beaten track but that wasn't always a good thing, or always the case either. I've already mentioned the problems we had moving our furniture and belongings into the house and we were to experience the same again when we left. However, we had a more potentially dangerous situation one morning an hour or two after I had left for the office. Sue was pottering around the cottage having had a leisurely bath after rising at a respectable hour, not having to work that day. The big log fire was making a good job of keeping the place warm and all was peaceful. Only the crackling of the fire could be heard above the normal sounds of the countryside.

Working in the kitchen, Sue realised that she could hear an unusual noise; a sort of roaring sound coming from the sitting room or, maybe from upstairs. She couldn't tell which, nor could she readily identify the sound. It might have been a low flying jet. She went out of the front door to investigate and was confronted by one of our farmer neighbours running up the lane, yelling, "Your chimney is on fire."

Sure enough, flames and smoke were spewing out of our chimney at a great rate of knots and it immediately became clear to Sue where her roaring noise was coming from.

The farmer had already called the Fire Brigade so there was not much that they could do but stand back and watch the display. After a short while they could hear the siren in the distance and watched as the fire engine raced along the road on the other side of the valley. The valley was quite steep at that point and the road zigzagged for a mile or so in order to negotiate the slopes. The Doppler effect of the siren echoed across to the assembled audience as the vehicle approached the spot opposite where they were standing and disappeared into the distance towards the junction which would lead to our hamlet. Time passed. Nothing appeared and they were astounded to see the fire engine again on the zigzag road across the valley; this time going in the opposite direction. Once again, the siren echoed across the valley.

By this time the flames and smoke had lessened in ferocity, Sue had checked inside to see that all was well and had come back out to talk to the, now gathering, crowd of neighbours. There was silence for a while, save for the sound of the fire, then came cheers from the crowd as the fire engine once again appeared on the road opposite going in the direction it was originally taking, still with siren blaring. Another few minutes passed and, as though triumphantly, the vehicle heaved into sight and stopped at the green. There were profuse apologies from the firemen. They had first gone to Mr and Mrs Ley's cottage at the bottom of the hill in the next hamlet, not Leys Cottage and they had not been clear where ours was. Moreover, the fire engine could not make the turn at the bottom of that hill and probably could not have made it up the narrow lane and steep hill between Eastdown and Churchill.

Anyway, Sue told them that the fire was as good as out by this time. However, they insisted that, now they were here, they should check it out anyway. They then discovered that they could not get the fire engine up our lane. Sue could have told them that in the first place. Not to be put off, they dispatched one man with a stirrup pump and a bucket up the lane to investigate.

Now to those of you too young to know what a stirrup pump is, I can tell you that it is a very antiquated piece of (at least) World War Two vintage fire fighting equipment. It consists of a pump, much like a slightly larger version of a bicycle tyre pump, attached to a metal stand with a stirrup shaped bit, which rests on the ground. The bottom end of the pump end goes in a bucket of water. You put your foot on the stirrup to steady the whole thing then pump like mad with one hand to produce a trickle of water through a small hose which you direct at the fire with the other. Maximum capacity was two gallons. Maximum pressure, well, it depended upon how strong the operator was! They were probably pretty effective for putting out waste paper basket fires but not much use for tackling burning houses, I suspect.

Anyway, I suppose it was better than nothing and our personal fireman, nearly as wide as he was tall, with an absurdly large, yellow fireman's helmet perched on his head, proceeded to check out the chimney fire. He did explain to Sue that, although the fire appeared to be out, there could be areas which might still be at risk. Our chimney was about five feet wide at the bottom tapering to about eight inches at the top. It was stone built at the base, changing to brick near the higher levels and it was still very, very hot. They could feel the heat in the upstairs rooms through which the chimney passed. The danger, the fireman said, was from timbers in the stonework near the chimney. Often they became so hot they would ignite even after the main source of the fire had gone out.

All was well, however, and the crew left happily advising us that, at least, we would not need to have the chimney swept for a while!

Thank heavens that fire, or any other, never took hold as we would have been at great risk due to the inability of the fire engine to get close enough to operate all its facilities. A good point to remember for future house purchases.

****

We were in Devon for the horrendous ice storms of 1982. Although we were once cut off from the outside world for four days, the magic sound of the tinkling of ice-covered branches and the sight of the sun glistening through the trees will always be in our minds and remind us of those days. Single blades and clumps of grass rose through the glistening ice fields looking like silver bluebells, and crystal chandeliers hung from the treetops, those that were not broken, that is.

Our cars were frozen solid to the ground, looking much like that old Colgate toothpaste advert where the tube is enclosed in an ice-cube. The freezing rain had made a "throw" of ice over the cars and draped to the ground. They were stuck solid for days due to long periods of freezing rain but it did not matter as all the narrow high-hedged roads were blocked anyway. The storm meant that I could not get into the office for four days and eventually only made it on a trailer hitched behind one of our farmer neighbour's four wheel drive tractors. We still have the photograph of our next-door neighbour and me sitting in the back of the farm trailer, on hay bales, bundled up in cold weather gear over our suits with briefcases on our knees. Such loyalty to our employers!

We were "trapped" in our hamlet often by snow. However, it didn't bother us too much, even when we lost electrical power for days on end. We had installed a bottled gas hob and had plenty of logs for the open fires and the solid fuel Rayburn to see us through.

One of our farmer neighbours still had to milk his cows even though the milk collection truck could not get through, so a couple of milk churns were left on the green for all of us to help ourselves.

We also had a good supply of candles, as one of our many finds in one of the outhouses on taking up residence, was a plastic barrel filled with half-burnt candles. As our predecessor in the cottage had worked in a local restaurant we assumed he had salvaged them from his place of work. We never ran out of emergency lighting!

The dozens of flickering candles, log fires blazing, the smell of wood smoke and a working stove and oven, courtesy of "Mr Rayburn" made our snow-bound episode a romantic and luxurious break.

It was in Devon just after we had married that Sue and I had our first experience of looking after animals other than dogs. We had borrowed "Teach Yourself Hens" from the library and had read up on how much to feed them, how many eggs we could expect from how many hens etc. We reckoned that six hens would supply us with enough eggs for ourselves, and some to spare. We expected to be able to sell the surplus, which would pay for their food.

Not quite self-sufficiency but some way towards it. Sue had always had ideas of more self-sufficiency. Perhaps a windmill, a thermal pond, solar panels or at least a decent sized vegetable garden.

Sue was away on a business trip in France when I collected six tiny, bald ex-battery hens in a crate from "Len the Hen" who was the local supplier of eggs at my office. Yes, bald, with clipped beaks, feet and wings, which certainly doesn't say anything positive about battery egg production.

Feeling as pleased as Tom from the TV sitcom "The Good Life", I brought them to their new home in our cottage garden. The poor shivering featherless creatures suddenly were to find themselves free, in a purpose-built run with their own hen house. You know, the wooden shack type, with a pitched roof, on cast iron wheels. A bit like an old beach hut. There was a roosting box along the length of one side and a ramp from ground level at one end up to the interior. The hen house was fully enclosed in a wired run, hopefully safe from foxes, and far enough away round the side of our cottage out of view, ear-shot and odour range! That afternoon I let them out of the crate and watched with great joy as they explored their new domain. After ensuring they had food and water I left them to enjoy their newfound freedom.

Later that night Sue telephoned from France and I told her of the additions to our "family". We went through the checklist on how to keep hens happy and she finally said:

"Did you put them in the hen house at dusk?"

"Of course not," I said, "the ramp door was open and I expected them to find their own way in."

Quick as flash, she said, "Well, just go and check that they have gone in and I'll call you back in a while to see how they are."

No rest for the wicked, I thought. There was nothing else for it but to brave the wind and rain outside, in my dressing gown. So out I went, torch in hand, to see what the hens were up to, half expecting to come across six mangled corpses. There were foxes in the area so I was a little worried at what I might find in the hen run. My fears were allayed when I found them all huddled, in the dark under the ramp, cold but safe. It did not take me too long to herd them all up the ramp, shut the door and return, dampened by my unexpected and uncomfortable errand, to the warmth of the log fire. A few minutes later the phone rang again. Sure enough, it was Sue.

I explained that all was well and that the hens did not put up much of a fight. They were now safe, locked in their new home.

"Did you make sure the hens were on their roosting rack inside the hen house?"

My reply was probably unprintable. Certainly, I have forgotten exactly what I said but it began along the lines of:

"If you think I'm going outside again tonight to tuck a few hens in their beds ...."

In the morning the hens were fine. They tumbled down the ramp like penguins and began pecking at the dirt as though they had been doing so all their short lives.

They soon gained feathers, became beautiful Rhode Island Reds and started to produce eggs. We put lighting on a timer in the hen house to improve production through the winter and they enjoyed the freedom of our garden for the rest of our stay in Devon. I did my bit for the environment by using shredded computer printouts from the office for the hen house litter and it composted very well for our vegetable garden.

One summer, Alice, one of our hens adopted our neighbour's brood of ducklings whose mother had disappeared - probably the work of a marauding fox. It was so strange seeing the hen strutting up and down the lane round the garden followed by a string of ducklings, not chicks. Even stranger when the ducklings took to the pond and the hen could only stand at the edge and wait for her brood to come ashore. The hen and the ducklings all remained firm friends, even when the ducklings became fully-grown.

Our cottage was in a hamlet, three farms, five or six houses or cottages, no pub, church or shops and well off the beaten tourist trail. The dogs all lived happily alongside the sheep, cows and other farm animals. As I mentioned, Sebbie was always in with the lambs and Sue was happy to help our neighbours out at lambing time. We didn't know it then but our lambing experiences would come in useful in later years in our house sitting "career", as you will see in due course.

On the darker side Spey, by being too friendly, accidentally crushed one of our neighbour's daughter's kittens - we were eventually forgiven - and we learned that Fisky, the spaniel, was a chocoholic. We only found this out one Easter when he ate a whole basket of Easter eggs and other chocolate "hidden" upstairs while we were out one day. I've never seen a dog drink so much water and I'll leave your imagination to picture the results the rest of that day and through the night. Not a pretty sight! Needless to say, he slept in one of the outhouses that night.

At the time I wasn't aware of the danger that "human" chocolate holds for dogs and cats. I am now. Apparently, the chemical theobromine, present in chocolate and harmless to humans, can cause vomiting, diarrhoea and convulsions in dogs. Fisky certainly suffered the first two, but thankfully not the third.

****

As ever, all good things tend to come to an end and it was with some trepidation that I received a phone call from the powers that be to ask whether I would accept another assignment, much sooner than I had expected, as I had been promised at least a couple of years in Devon. However, when they said the new position was in St. Louis, Missouri in the USA, my first reaction was to jump at the chance, although our expected stay in Devon would be cut short. We had been to the States on holiday many times but this was to undertake a three year task based right in the heart of the country and I could see the opportunity for travel and experiences that we could never have on short trips from Britain.

But if I were to take the job, what would become of our dogs? It immediately became obvious to us that Spey, Sebbie, and Fisky could not go with us - if only because of the "prison sentence" (quarantine) which they would have to undergo on their return to our rabies-free shores at the end of their stay. We also had no idea of exactly where we would be living, what sort of house, flat or whatever in which we would stay and so, reluctantly, we began to seek out alternatives for the dogs if we opted for the move.

Family was the obvious answer and we managed to convince my parents to take Spey, Sue's mother to take Sebbie and my sister to have Fisky, the spaniel. No, I don't know why the dog was given that name, perhaps her previous owner couldn't spell Frisky - we'll never know.

With the dogs' future assured we could see no reason why we should not accept the exciting prospect of three years in a "foreign" country. It would be a good career move for me and although Sue would have to leave an interesting job it seemed too good an opportunity to miss, so I accepted the offer.

I must tell you that by this time, our ex-battery hens had been given a Christmas present by our neighbours in the shape of a magnificent cockerel, which we named Winston, as we lived in the hamlet called Churchill. I never fancied the eggs much after Winston arrived. No real reason! Sue laughs about it to this day, but they just did not seem the same. To complete the hens' story, on our departure from Devon we gave them to our neighbours to roam free-range with their own hens. We felt good about the fact that we had liberated the hens from battery cage conditions into an open hen run and they would spend the rest of their days running free range with many others. At least they had had a far better life than before they met up with us and we had enjoyed unlimited "free" eggs during our stay.

Just before our departure from Devon we approached our neighbours and asked if they would mind if we held a farewell party in their farmyard. To our delight, they said that they were planning one for us anyway, so we combined our efforts and resources. We borrowed a huge rectangular marquee that just fitted the farmyard with the guys secured to various outbuildings. This effectively formed a complete roof over the farmyard yet still allowed access to the barns. Mike, our neighbour, spread sand on the uneven cobbled farmyard and we built a plywood floor over the entire area. We had a bar planned for one barn, a live band in another, barbecue in a third and salads etc in yet another. The large tent was for sitting out and dancing.

The arrangements were all well in hand and over a hundred people had accepted our invitations. It was early September in 1983 and the weather looked perfect when we had our rehearsal the night before. Well, beer needs sampling doesn't it? And, after all, we did have several barrels lined up. We sat there with the fairy lights glowing on a typical warm, end of summer evening, thinking how it was a perfect time and place for our farewell party. It was a wonderful evening and the stars twinkled peacefully in a clear sky above us. We congratulated ourselves on our preparations and looked forward to a successful evening the following day.

Just before we went to bed that night, with growing apprehension we watched the late weather forecast on TV. The weatherman said that unexpected hurricane force winds and heavy rains were sweeping in from the west and would be upon us by the following nightfall. During the following day several of our guests phoned in to ask whether the party was still on and we of course said, yes. How could we cancel? Everything was organised; food, drink, the band, the whole nine yards and who can trust the weather forecast anyway?

The day wore on. From starting out as a perfect September late summer's day the sky became dark and threatening and then the winds started to blow. We secured canvas walls to the marquee where the interior was exposed in the gaps between the barns. The tent pegs and guys were re-checked and polythene sheeting was strategically placed in case of driving rain. The guests started to arrive, the beer and wine flowed, the music played and then it rained. It rained and it blew - hard.

Our impromptu flooring sagged a little where the water swept down the lane and washed away most of our sand base. We slackened shrinking guy ropes as they became wet and gusts were lifting the two six inch diameter tent poles a good eight inches off the floor. Canvas was billowing in the wind and rain was blowing through all apertures. A trip to the loo in our house or our neighbour's became an adventure and meant a soaking, but no one cared. The noise was horrendous but still the party went on. The guests were wet, the dogs were wet but everyone was having a great time.

The rain worsened. So much so, that the band had to stop playing for fear of electrocution as the rain was pouring through the old tiled roof of the barn and on to their equipment. However, a local old timer produced an accordion and the party continued well into the small hours. Having experienced that party I can well understand the hurricane party mentality of some residents of Florida and the Caribbean. Not that I think it is sensible to ignore evacuation advice or orders but partying under extreme weather conditions does have a certain buzz about it.

We are sure that our party is still a source of discussion in Churchill and the surrounding area. Whenever we visit our friends there, and we do as often as we can, we reminisce about the happenings that night. We recall that it was the same evening that the Bristol Flower Show marquees were blown down. Later, the weathermen likened it to a full hurricane and we considered ourselves really lucky that our soiree ended up with nothing more serious than a few wet and muddy people with well-earned hangovers the next day.

Regretfully, the day after the party we began packing our boxes and organized our furniture to go into storage. Sue and my sister, Raine, soon realized that as we couldn't send any remaining alcohol into store (well, not any that might go off) or in our boxes, it had to go. The pair soon discovered that cornflakes and Baileys, coffee with Baileys and ice cream with Baileys could soon cure a hangover!

Sadly, all too soon, we said our farewells to our many good friends and neighbours in Churchill and its surrounds to set off for the "Colonies".

I'll cover a lot more about our stay in the USA, later.

****

The three years passed all too quickly. We missed our dogs but occasionally we did look after friends' pets in the USA as you'll see. When we returned to England we expected to resume our ownership of the four-legged friends we had left behind. However, my parents had become so attached to Spey and my sister to Fisky that they both asked to keep them. How could we say no? My parents had relished the company. Spey was added security for them and, perhaps more importantly, he had made them take more exercise than perhaps they might, had they not had a large dog to care for. Moreover, by that time, my sister had had Fisky longer than we had owned him.

On the other hand, Sue's mother was more than ready to hand Sebbie back to us and so at least we had the company of one of the three. Sue was greeted with open arms by her mother and on opening hers for the hug, Sebbie was thrust into them with, "and here's your dog back"!

She added, "Dogs are such a tie to a socializing lady of a 'certain age'".

We were happy in the knowledge that Spey and Fisky had good homes and that we still had frequent contact with them, as they were both with family who lived within regular visiting distance.

On our return from America I was working in London and we lived in Biggin Hill, Kent from where I commuted into the city. The chances of working overseas again were slim, so we "rescued" Lucy, another cocker spaniel - just to keep Sebbie company, (if you remember, he thinks he's a spaniel). My work was in a central London office managing a large defence contract with the Government of Saudi Arabia. Although I visited Saudi occasionally, I had no inkling that circumstances would soon change and that our home life would again be disrupted by the offer of employment in foreign parts.

I had only been working in London for just over a year when, tragically, my opposite number in Riyadh was killed in a car crash and I received a phone call from "head office" asking whether I would be willing to take his place at short notice. This came only eighteen months after returning from St. Louis so we had to think hard about going overseas again for what was to be a two and a half year assignment.

Again, the dogs came high on the list of factors to be considered in the decision-making process and we were grateful that my parents offered to take Sebbie who would then be reunited with his old friend Spey, the Labrador. My sister, an avid dog lover, again came to the rescue and volunteered to have our new spaniel, Lucy.

At the end of a long and latterly very happy life, Fisky had come to the end of the road a few months earlier. So, with our canine family again in the care of our real family we set off for our unexpected trip to the desert.

For one reason or another, our planned, relatively short, stay in Saudi turned into six and a half years. If we had known that at the outset, we may well have acquired a dog during our stay or at least taken Sebbie with us. We came home at least twice a year and saw our dogs each time and that they were just as well looked after and happy as they could have been with us. However, during our extended absence both the now elderly Sebbie the poodle and Spey the lab had died and our spaniel Lucy who had now been with my sister far longer than with us had contracted diabetes. Star that she was, my sister almost demanded that she be allowed to continue to care for Lucy. We agreed, offering to share the costs of the drugs required (an injection a day for life) and the special food to make life as comfortable as possible for Lucy's remaining years. Taking a urine sample first thing in the morning every day in all weathers to determine blood/sugar level deserves a medal in its own right. Especially when it involved following a female dog around, carrying a ladle, trying catch the first pee of the day, often in cold, wet and windy conditions!

I relate all this to try to show the reader (more than singular, I hope) that Sue and I are dog lovers and as long as we are physically able will always have, or be around, dogs of any size, shape or breed.

After taking early retirement on my return from Saudi Arabia we agreed that we wanted to do a good deal of travelling. We therefore reluctantly decided that it would not be a good idea to start a "family" again, so to speak, and therefore abandoned the idea of dogs of our own until we felt we should "settle down".

So when we had only been home in Yorkshire for a couple of months and an acquaintance of my sister's, living in East Sussex, was let down by her house/dog sitter it was suggested that we might fill the gap at short notice. And so, to coin a phrase, that's how it all began.

Chapter Two

In Foreign "Fields"

Before getting into relating the ups and downs of our "dog's life" I must record a word or two about our experiences in the United States of America and Saudi Arabia. It would require another whole book to go into much detail about all our many and varied experiences and travels. I must therefore restrict myself to a few short items where dogs or other animals feature that might be fitting for a book such as this.

My work in St Louis, Missouri was a three year assignment and we decided that owning pets was not an option, partly, as I have already mentioned, because of the Draconian quarantine laws on our return to England but also because of our desire to travel at every opportunity whilst we were in the States.

However, many of our neighbours owned dogs and we soon had the chance to look after some of them while their owners were "out of town".

Pete was a delightful Cockerpoo (a cocker spaniel/poodle cross for the uninitiated), and belonged to a neighbour and new friend of ours. Pete had been given to her as a present by her family, to be both a companion and guard dog. The only problem was, she worked full time and lived in a smallish condominium, with no private garden. So Sue, on meeting Pete and his owner shortly after they moved in down the hall, offered to look after him during the working day. Now that was OK in theory, but Pete was supposed to be a guard dog and his owner left for work long before Sue arose from her bed. This meant that Pete had to be collected from his home at a more respectable hour. The first few times were fraught to say the least!

On first unlocking and opening of Pete's condo door a black bundle of fur, barking wildly and growling with teeth bared, hurled itself at the door as it swung open. Sue shut the door quickly. Now what was she to do? Quietly, but in an authoritative manner, she talked to Pete through the closed door. After a while she re-opened it, this time more slowly, only to shut it again quickly as the black tornado re-launched itself teeth first at the opening. Right, she thought, we will do this quickly and stand well back. Throwing the door wide open, she jumped behind the jamb, prepared to fight off an irate guard dog. But no, Pete ignored her completely, tore off down the hall to our own front door and, pushing the door open he ran right in!

On her hurried, breathless arrival a minute or so behind him, there was Pete, curled up on our bed and looking quite at home. I should say that Pete had spent some time in our condo in the company of his owner prior to Sue's first solo day with him so I suppose he came to consider it as his second home. This scenario was replayed each time Sue looked after him and he never learned to greet her with a wagging tail! Always protective of his territory, I guess.

However, Pete had lots of character and once away from his own territory, was an extremely friendly dog. His other noteworthy quirk was of a far more gourmet flavour.

Although we had no private gardens around our condominium we did have a large communal area of landscaping. There were manicured gardens at the front and lawns and flowerbeds backed onto woods at the rear of the building. Pete's owner had planted a few tomatoes and we watched them flower and produce small green fruits. Slowly, over the summer, the green tomatoes grew larger and started to turn red. We all eagerly awaited the first ripe tomatoes from these home grown plants. But we waited and we waited. We watched them grow to quite a size and start to turn but none seemed to ripen completely.

At last it struck us that someone was harvesting them before we could. Who was the thief? We kept our eyes peeled but no one seemed to go near them. Very odd, we thought. Then one morning, as Sue let Pete run outside he disappeared around the building and out of sight. Sue chased after him and lo and behold, she had caught the tomato thief! There was Pete happily pulling the ripening tomatoes from the plants and chewing them in the long grass under the trees! He must have needed something vital in his diet that only tomatoes have! Presumably it wasn't only country singer John Denver who had a liking for Home Grown Tomatoes!

Whilst on the subject of dogs with unusual tastes I must mention that Sue's Sebbie was the only dog I ever knew who liked watercress. Couldn't get enough of it! Most dogs eat apples but he also had a liking for pears. We also knew a spaniel whose favourite treat was freshly sliced cucumber. In mid afternoon he would paw at the refrigerator door until he was given his daily treat. In fact it soon became the norm for him to expect half a slice every time the fridge door was opened. Later on we were to meet a golden retriever puppy that ate rose hips and plums. Not only windfalls. She would get up on her hind legs and pluck them from the tree!

Back to the script! We also had other dog visitors, either by arrangement or ones who just dropped in. The word must have gone around the canine community. Sam, a peek-a-poo, yes, half poodle half Pekinese, was a regular visitor from next door. He had an endearing habit of getting so excited he would run round and round after his tail. A little, no, a lot like Dougal in The Magic Roundabout, for those who might remember the children's television programme. Although designed mainly for younger children, we suspect many mature people might have watched the tail end waiting for the six o'clock evening news to start!

Another mixed breed pooch used to pop and see us, although we never worked out what he was or where he came from. He was tiny and longhaired. One day he arrived looking like a badly decorated Christmas tree. He had been rummaging in the woods and was covered head to tail in king-size burrs. He could hardly move as they were under his legs, in his ears and covered his long tail. They were everywhere. He was most uncomfortable and sat outside our door looking very unhappy. We took out our dog brush and scissors and well over an hour later we had a happier more comfortable dog but he now looked like a Swiss cheese! We often wondered what on earth his owner thought when he returned home.

One of our pre-arranged canine visitors, a cocker spaniel called Charlotte, came at short notice one Halloween. Both her owners worked for an airline and had been called out suddenly. They asked if we would have Charlotte overnight. Sue explained that we were going to a Halloween party, but of course Charlotte could come and stay. Bruce said he would drop her off on their way to the airport. We went ahead and dressed in our costumes for our Halloween party.

The front door bell rang and Sue went out of our condo down the hall and up the stairs to collect Charlotte. As she opened the door Bruce took one look, grabbed hold of Charlotte and headed off back towards his car.

Sue called after him, "What's wrong?"

Bruce stopped, turned around and with a shame-faced look came back saying, "Oh, it's you."

What Sue had forgotten was that she was dressed as a punk rocker complete with face paint, spiked hair and black plastic bin bag dress! We have both laughed about it many times since.

We never quite became used to the extremes of weather in St Louis (pronounced Lewis, by the way, and not Louie as many Brits annoyingly refer to it). It could be uncomfortably hot and humid in the summer and dangerously cold in the winter.

By hot, I mean summer time temperatures in the hundreds Fahrenheit with almost one hundred per cent humidity to match. I'm talking about real, sweltering, wet, uncomfortable, shirt-soaking heat. "Thank the Lord for air-conditioning," I often said.

There was no way we could have lived comfortably without air conditioning in our homes, cars and offices. How the early settlers survived I don't know. I suppose many of them didn't! Don't suppose they could have air-conditioned horse drawn wagons anyway! They were tougher people in those days I guess. Bit like our predecessors in Britain who lived without central heating.

Talking of weather, there are two things about the US weather forecasting and the seasons I could never get used to.

Firstly, am I the only person in the world who cannot stand American weather forecasters talking about hot and cold temperatures? I'll accept hot or cold weather, yes. But surely, temperatures can only be high or low?

Secondly, we could never understand why Americans are so fanatical about the start and end dates of summer, winter, hurricane season etc. They always seem so surprised if a hurricane dares to spawn in the Atlantic or Gulf of Mexico after the end of the season. And why do swimming pools always open on a certain date, despite the weather and close at the end of the season when everyone knew that the hot weather always lasted for a few more weeks?

As for the cold in St Louis, I'm talking about really dangerous, bone-chilling cold. The lowest temperature we experienced was minus fifteen degrees Fahrenheit, around minus twenty six degrees Centigrade in new money. It was so cold, that exposed skin would freeze in a matter of minutes. Like many others we had thought that St Louis was in the deep south but in fact it is only a couple of hundred miles or so south of Chicago.

It was so cold on occasions that the chimney in our ground floor (of three floors) condominium would not draw due to the amount of freezing cold air stacked in the chimney above the fire grate. The only way we found we could produce an updraft in those circumstances was to hold an electric hairdryer at the bottom of the shaft for a few minutes before attempting to light the fire. Once a warm updraft had been established it would get going with ease and our huge log fire would produce enough heat to keep out the cold and boost our central heating system.

We have come across this phenomenon in the UK but, as we don't often experience such low temperatures here, far less so than in the deep mid-west State of Missouri.

Another unusual but very useful function we found for the hairdryer was to thaw out the ice on the French windows leading to our patio, allowing us to go outside on even the coldest days to fire up the barbecue. Yes, even in the dead of winter, more often than not we'd cook outside. Coated and gloved I'd go out for a few minutes, arrange the charcoal, pour on and light the fluid and rush back in.

A little while later I'd go back out, spread the coals and put the cooking grid back on. Through the window I'd check when the coals were ready and brave the cold once again to throw on the steaks, chops or whatever and supervise from the warmth of our sitting room. I'd venture outside at least once more to turn things over and then a final trip to retrieve the meat and close things down. We thought nothing of it but we did get some strange looks from some of our neighbours who never even cooked inside all year round, let alone outside in the winter.

Mentioning our patio and the French windows reminds me of the time one summer evening whilst we were sitting in our "great room" eating dinner, when we saw a frog emerge from our log pile outside the French windows. It began to hop across the patio, obviously enjoying feeding on insects after an earlier shower of rain. As we watched, a largish snake appeared and before we could intervene it seized the frog in its mouth and proceeded to swallow it. Not that we would have intervened anyway as there were a good few venomous snakes in that part of Missouri and our powers of reptile recognition were not too far advanced at that time.

I can still picture today the frog's legs disappearing into the snake's mouth. Of course we just happened to be eating Spaghetti Bolognese! We couldn't face the rest of our meal after that episode and forever after, whenever we have that particular dish we think of that evening and the hapless frog.

We have always loved to travel and did so in the United States at every opportunity.

During our stay in St Louis on one of our holidays we drove 6,500 miles from Missouri through Oklahoma along Route 66, or what was left of it, out to New Mexico and Arizona. We took in the Grand Canyon and a lot of other not so grand canyons, but just as beautiful. We toured through California and Utah and then up to Wyoming and Montana. From there we drove east through the Dakotas and then south through Nebraska and back to Missouri, an amazing journey. Considering we did it in seventeen days we still managed to take in most of the major attractions on the way. Although that trip is a story in its own right I thought that here I'd record just a few notable experiences, some animal oriented, which were of interest along the way.

We'd travelled through some backcountry in deepest Wyoming, real way out west territory, beautiful rolling scenery and of course, big sky. Or was that Montana? Anyway, we rolled into a sleepy town somewhere just west of Billings and stopped for gas. They would not have understood the word petrol, so I thought I'd better write in an American accent here just to keep it ethnically correct and to set the scene.

33

As we pulled into the gas station we noticed a dog lying in the shade under the trunk of the Sheriff's car. It was a hot dusty day, the sort when you're real glad that the car has air-conditioning and you're carrying a cooler in the car full of iced drinks. (I can't say beer here as it's illegal to transport alcohol over some state borders.) We commented to the gas station attendant - no self-service machines here, they might not even have had electricity - that the town was pretty quiet.

"Yeah," he said, "we ain't had nothing major happen here since the sheriff's dog was run over crossin' the road a while back."

We weren't surprised and hoped that nobody was about to dial 911 (999 in English) as another "deputy" dog might be biting the dust if the sheriff reversed his car without looking underneath.

I'd just remarked to Sue that this looked like the original one-horse town when, right on cue, around the corner came a single horse pulling an ancient buggy - looking as if it came right of the set of Bonanza or The Ponderosa. The garage attendant just shook his head as we fell about laughing.

A little further on we saw an old bloodhound fast asleep on a rickety old rocking chair perched on an equally old and rickety porch. It was good to see that there are parts of America which have as yet escaped the hustle and bustle of the majority of fast-track USA.

On our journey we marvelled at the many fantastic sights along the way. Just to have travelled the old Route 66 with all its romantic names like Amarillo, Albuquerque, Winslow and Flagstaff was a great thrill. They are all still there and proud of it. Some of the diners advertised the old route along the way and a few of the hamburgers tasted that old as well

We visited the Petrified Forest, Walnut Canyon, Sunset Crater, the Grand Canyon and the Painted Desert in Arizona. Just north, in Utah we took in Zion and Bryce

Canyons, not as mind boggling in size as the Grand Canyon but all beautiful in their own right. We remember Zion notably for its depth, sheer cliffs and waterfalls and Bryce because of its amazing rock formations topped by an icing of snow and spectacular colours, particularly around sunset.

We spent one night in Las Vegas, the only place on our journey where we had made a prior hotel reservation, at Circus Circus. It took us four hours to lose one hundred dollars, big money in those days, and we were strong willed enough to walk away from the tables after reaching our pre-set limit. What an experience, but I could not see us ever spending a couple of weeks, or more, gambling there as many punters do.

On to California, where, among many beautiful sights, we saw Yosemite, the magnificent Giant Sequoia trees and took the famous scenic nine mile drive through Carmel, where Clint Eastwood had just taken over as mayor. Unfortunately, it was Sunday and he wasn't in his office. We travelled the '49er trail in California, visited a few of the old mines like Sutter's Mill and pondered on the many thousands who rushed to the area to seek their fortune and recalled that most of them didn't find it. All those old country songs came to life as we visited the places about which many of them had been written.

Pebble Beach golf course was beautiful but we didn't stop to play, couldn't get a mortgage! Sue's cousin Pete, once played there. He had told us that he was not long into his round when it started to rain as hard as only it can in hot climates. It was throwing it down. However, Pete had paid a small fortune for his game of golf at the fabled course and, like a true Yorkshireman, was going to finish his round come what may. My apologies, Pete, I know you are a Teessider but for this tale you either had to come from Yorkshire or, dare I say it, Scotland?

In addition, due to the weather forecast, he had also purchased some very expensive waterproof clothing in the

Pro Shop prior to teeing off. His caddie (compulsory equipment at Pebble Beach) was furious and wanted to walk-in at the sixth hole but they eventually made it to the nineteenth soaking wet but happy. At least, Phil was. I never asked him his score.

We didn't quite leave our hearts in San Francisco but we could see what the songwriter meant. We jumped a tram, didn't have a chance to pay, and travelled the steep streets you always see in movie car chases. Our seafood lunch on Fisherman's Wharf was delicious – a must if you ever get to the Golden Gate city. It certainly was a wonderful lively town but what a contrast was the sight of the now disused prison of Alcatraz, lying ominously foreboding out in the bay.

Yellowstone Park was amazing and our stay there alone would have been worth the whole 6,500-mile journey. We arrived at the park just as they opened the westernmost gate for the season. There was still deep snow on the ground and all the other gates were still closed. This meant that we almost had the place to ourselves, and cars, vans and four by fours had not yet outnumbered the animals as they tended to do later in the year. The mountains, two of them at least 10,000 feet above sea level, rose majestically from the plains and rivers. Their flanks and tops still carpeted by glistening pure white winter snow.

The hot springs and rivers steamed in the crisp, clear, cool mountain air and the geyser Old Faithful was, at that time, still erupting every twenty six minutes or so. One of our lasting memories was of the many bison, encrusted with snow and ice formed by steam frozen on their pelts as they stood keeping warm by the warm waters in the hot springs.

We stayed the night in "the largest log cabin in the world", The Old Faithful Lodge, complete with squirrels in the dining room. A truly magnificent part of the country and we vowed to return one day.

One lunchtime we came upon a town in the middle of nowhere whose name we could not pronounce. We pulled into a diner and heatedly discussed throughout the meal the many possible ways the name could be said and we could not reach agreement. On the way out, whilst paying our bill, I said to the girl on the cash desk, "Could you please tell us, very slowly, the name of the place we are at?"

She obviously thought we were foreigners and a little slow with our understanding of American English, so without blinking an eyelid, she very carefully said, "B-u-r-g-e-r K-i-n-g." Well, we were too polite to laugh in front of her but we could hardly contain ourselves until we were outside the restaurant when we fell about laughing and had great difficulty getting the car open and driving off through our tears of laughter.

No, I can't deceive the honest reader! That didn't actually happen to us and I am trying to keep this book as close to the truth as I can. I haven't even applied for my poetic license yet.

However, what did happen all too frequently was the inevitable comment, "gee, you sure do he-ave a ke-ute accent". We had put up with this for many years and eventually we occasionally but politely responded with, "No, we don't have an accent, you do."

It's very apparent that Americans, particularly in places where foreigners rarely go, will often listen to how you are saying something and not to what you are saying. This inevitably would result in the ubiquitous, "'Scuse me?" and necessitate repeating the whole thing. You try going into a store in the mid-west and asking for a tin of "tomahtoes". They won't have a clue.

Just across the Montana border into Wyoming we arrived at the small town of Sheridan. Now Sheridan is a very small western town and its only claim to fame as far as we knew was that not long before we got into town "The Artiste Formerly Known as Prince" had stayed there. Before that nobody had ever heard of it. Apparently, one of

37

the town residents had won a national competition for a date with the pop singer and he had kept his part of the bargain, bringing instant recognition to this hitherto sleepy neck of the woods.

One lasting memory of the town was our visit to a large pawnshop shop which sprawled on one side of the dusty main street behind an old hitching rail. When I'm relating this episode verbally I have to be careful not to use the other spelling of pawn as it was not that kind of store. Anyway, once in the shop, I went over to a bunch of guitars hanging on a wall and was browsing happily when I was approached by the proprietor, a contented looking, white haired, elderly guy.

"D' yuh play, son?" he asked.

"Well, I try", I said, picking up a guitar. He took another off the wall. We found a couple of rocking chairs and then spent a good hour running through some of the early rock and roll numbers and a good few blues songs. It was the right place for it and he was just what you might have expected in a town like that. A laid back old-time guitar picker with all the time in the world to indulge in his music, right in that part of the country where it seemed most appropriate. Nice place, Sheridan.

We stopped one night in Mammoth Springs Motel in Hot Springs in South Dakota. It was only when we explored the local area that evening that we found out the significance of the name. During land development a few years before our visit, builders had uncovered several mammoth skeletons. Work had been halted whilst the site was excavated and an astonishing number of whole and part skeletons had been found.

Apparently there had been a huge water hole on the site many thousands of years before and the sloping sides were so steep that many animals had not been able to climb out and had perished on the spot. A huge air-conditioned timber and glass building had been erected over the whole area and excavation at the lower levels was still underway.

A wooden staircase and walkway had been constructed allowing the public close access to all levels and clever use of lighting clearly showed how the "graveyard" had evolved over the centuries. What a sight! Apparently, at that time, this was the largest and most complete collection of mammoth remains found anywhere in the world.

The Devil's Tower in Wyoming (shades of ET) and those immortal past presidents carved into Mount Rushmore just across the border in South Dakota seemed tame after Yellowstone but were a must see. And see them we did, on our southward journey down through Kansas City and back to St Louis.

If I've whetted your appetite to take a similar trip, or even a small part of it, I have achieved my objective here. There is so much more to do and see in the United States of America than trips to Florida and the other run of the mill tourist attractions. Although, don't get me wrong, they too are well worth a visit!

The American people are so hospitable, generous and welcoming as well, particularly, again if you stray off the beaten track. We were up in Northern California one time and coming to the end of our travelling day looking for a place to stay the night. We happened upon the small town of Elk's Cove, right on the coast and spotted a bed and breakfast place. Now, B&Bs in the USA are not like ours in England. The average B&B in the UK is a room in a farmhouse or other large house with bedrooms to spare. Mostly, a bathroom would be shared with other guests and although things are usually clean and tidy, they sometimes can be a bit primitive. Of course, this is reflected in the price as most B&Bs in the UK cost but a fraction of those in the USA. I know some out there will disagree and of course, there are exceptions but even those dissenters might agree that generally the foregoing is true.

We pulled up outside our chosen B&B, went in and enquired about accommodation.

"I'm afraid I only have one room left," the owner said, "would you like to take a look?"

Thinking the worst, as the best rooms usually get taken first, we traipsed along behind her to investigate our prospective home for the night. Along behind us came her two dogs, a large long- haired German shepherd and a wire-haired terrier. She opened the room door and we looked in. Well, if this was her worst room we should certainly have liked to have seen her best! Spacious and very tastefully furnished it had a superb view of the gardens and the sea. On a side table was a full bowl of various exotic fruits complemented by a half bottle of wine and the same of port. We gladly agreed to take the room and fetched our gear from the car.

After settling in we returned to reception on our way out, wanting to explore the beach and cliffs before sunset. On our way through we asked the owner if we could take her dogs for a walk on the beach.

With a straight face she said, "No, you cannot."

We must have looked crestfallen, and she immediately continued, "They will take you."

Sure enough, the dogs led us through the garden, past a pergola which looked strangely familiar, down a steep cliff path, which we might not have found on our own, and onto the broad expanse of beach. We threw sticks for the dogs, explored the caves, examined shells and driftwood and enjoyed getting rid of the stiffness inevitably incurred by driving most of the day. We picked up a piece of driftwood, whittled by countless waves, looking remarkably like a shark. It still sits in our bathroom at home, a memento of one of our many journeys.

Nothing like a good stiff walk on a beach and all that sea air to build up an appetite for a beer or two and a good dinner! The dogs loved it – the walk, that is, not the beers and dinner - and so, of course, did we! The north California coastline is beautiful at the best of times but this part was stunning. When we looked back at the evocative photos of that Victorian gingerbread house, the misty, sea-sprayed beach, and the sun setting over the garden, we suddenly realised why it was so familiar. It had been featured in a recent National Geographic Magazine article. That was the very article which had sent us to that part of California. Fate had led us there.

Having enthused about the country, there are some pretty boring parts of America too, particularly the long stretches across the plains, seemingly endless highways and destinations are far, very far, apart. That said, by far the best means of travel is by road - if one has the time. If you are going, get off the highways and explore the old towns, talk to people who don't often see foreigners. They, and you, will love it and you'll never forget your experiences along the way.

****

For the same reasons we considered before setting off for the United States of America we decided not to have pets whilst we were in Saudi Arabia. Although we did adopt a few cats along the way and we nearly had a dog, as we shall see.

The Saudis rarely kept dogs as pets as they were seen to be unclean and were usually only kept for hunting or guard dog purposes. However, many of our diplomat friends and some longer-term ex-patriots had dogs whose company we often enjoyed - the human element as well as their dogs!

We spent many pleasant hours getting away from the city out in the desert in our four-wheel drive vehicles. The dogs were able to run free and it was a delight to watch them. Camping overnight far from the city lights was a special treat on some of the cooler weekends of the year. If you have never seen a desert night sky without any intrusion from clouds, city lights or sound, you have not seen the universe at its best.

There are very few places in Britain where one can get far enough away from civilisation to encounter complete silence and experience such awe inspiring views. In England there always seems to be a bird, rustling leaves or trees moving in the breeze or the faint hum of some road or other in the distance. Light pollution at night rarely allows us to view the sky in all its glory.

However, fifty miles into the Arabian Desert there was no such intrusion. The only human instigated encroachments were the occasional high altitude jet aircraft passing overhead or one of the many satellites crossing the vast empty sky. They were acceptable but not as spectacular as the ever-present falling stars, their incandescent trails glittering behind them on their doomed voyages through the atmosphere.

Even in the heat of the day, once car engines were silenced the quietness had to be experienced to be believed. That far off the beaten track, even the inevitable desert flies took a while to find us. At night the silence was deafening.

Far from being only flat uninteresting expanses of sand, the desert was a never-ending series of completely different landscapes. Some areas would contain the traditional shifting sands with huge dunes, hundreds of feet high, moving with the desert winds and never staying in the same place for long. Other areas reminded us of Arizona with huge escarpments and pillars of rock rising from the desert floor. John Wayne would certainly have felt at home there. The escarpment, only a short drive to the west of Riyadh, provided a dramatic vista of the desert below, stretching as far as the eye could see.

The vast Empty Quarter, known as Rub el Khali, to the south west of the country, covers an area into which the whole of England would fit with room to spare. Only the Bedouin, the foolhardy, or the very experienced and well-equipped travellers venture far into this vast, desolate area.

We kept well clear. Some Westerners didn't, and one or two didn't make it back. Even when travelling only a short distance from the city it was unwise to venture out in only one vehicle, particularly in the summer. The desert was a beautiful, haunting place but like the ocean, could be calm and peaceful one minute but unleash its power the next. If you've ever seen a sand storm you'll know what I mean. You could be enjoying a pleasant day relaxing in the peace and quiet when you'd see in the distance a smudge on the horizon. The smudge would grow into a wall, then to a gigantic cloud several hundred feet high. From a dead calm you'd hear and feel the wind accelerate from a breeze to a strong wind and finally, a storm force gale. Then the sand would be upon you.

As thick as the thickest fog but this stuff hurt! You couldn't see a yard in front of your face but then you didn't want to open your eyes anyway. If you've ever been on a sandy beach in a very strong wind you might begin to understand as you will have felt the sand biting your ankles. Increase the wind strength to gale force then imagine the sand hitting every part of your body. It got into your mouth, your eyes, and your ears; up your nose and down your neck. The only thing to do was to get into your car and wait it out. If you had a car, that is.

The camels would lie down, backs to the wind, with their tails between their legs and their heads likewise at the other end. Their Bedouin owners would squat on the lee side of the camels, huddled under their thobes, gutteras and bernoose until the storm had passed.

Things weren't much better in the city either. Traffic would come to a standstill. The sand would get in to our houses under the doors through the window frames. Little piles would accumulate and there would be a fine layer of dust everywhere, even in the cupboards. One interesting sight was you were able to look at the sun nearly obliterated by the sand but clearly enough to see the sunspots with the naked eye.

The landscape around the Capital, Riyadh, contained a wealth of archaeological interest. We found many shells and fossils of coral and other sea creatures high on the escarpment to the west of the city, even a fossilised sea urchin. Plain evidence that the whole continent was at one time deep under the ocean. In addition, not far from the city there was an area where great chunks of petrified wood lay on the sand. Huge trees at one time had flourished in the middle of this arid, harsh land.

I say arid, but only water was required to bring the desert to life. Each year during the first rains the desert could be seen to change colour. Driving between Riyadh and Dhahran at certain times of the year the whole landscape would be covered in a thin carpet of green.

About thirty miles from Riyadh there was a large valley completely covered in little blue irises. They only appeared once a year for a few days and then only flowered in the early morning so it was quite an event on our calendar and many expatriates made the trip to see this wonder of nature.

We did our bit for the ecology during our stay. We moved house several times and three of those moves were to new houses with virgin sand as gardens. It took much hard work and more than a little expense but three times we transformed the sand in our gardens into little green oases. Seed and grass plugs brought in from Florida grew extremely quickly and eucalyptus trees in particular, thrived in the sand given sufficient water.

We planted one gum tree around six feet tall and within eighteen months it had more than tripled in size. It wasn't long in any of our new gardens before the grass, trees and plants brought in the insects, lizards and birds. Well, some insects and lizards were there already but butterflies and bees appeared from nowhere and migrating birds used our shade as a respite from the scorching sun. When you've been away from good British lawns for a while it is amazing how quickly you realise that you take them for granted when you have them, and how much you miss them when they are not there. Just to walk barefoot on damp grass was a great pleasure and our cats loved it too.

Surprising also, how much of a temperature drop could be achieved by introducing vegetation into an otherwise desolate landscape.

Nothing to do with dogs or animals but I must mention the desert concerts. Every once in a while a concert would be organised to take place at a secret location way out in the desert under the stars. As gatherings involving members of the opposite sex were strictly forbidden, preparations and the events themselves had to be kept very low-key. On the appointed afternoons many four-wheel drive vehicles could be seen leaving Riyadh for the desert and would arrive at the concert venues in time to set up for a picnic and to await the evening's entertainment.

There was never anything so grand as an orchestra or band but by clever positioning of a generator and powerful hi-fi and compact disc equipment, the sound and atmosphere was enthralling under the desert sky. The venues were invariably in "horseshoe" canyons with the sound source set up on the desert floor facing the horseshoe with the audience arranged around the canyon walls on ledges, which provided natural amphitheatres. Candles and lanterns completed the picture, flickering in the darkness whilst music such as the 1812 Overture or Ravel's Bolero echoed around the canyons.

There was always a dog or two on our desert "safaris" and we were often aware that there were also packs of wild dogs on the fringes of the city. Most of these were feral having been dumped by their owners at some time or other and were to be avoided for obvious reasons.

One day Sue found two small puppies outside our compound gates and being the way she is, could not leave them abandoned by their mother to die in the sun. She brought them in and we fed them until they gained their strength. They looked very much like Labrador puppies so we advertised among the ex-pat population for someone to take them in. We eventually found homes for both of them, one to good friends of ours. Later we felt more than a little embarrassed when their "Labrador" turned into a large gangly, extremely disobedient, desert dog. By desert dog I mean a cross between everything but shaped much like a saluki. However, our friends loved him so that was all that mattered and they did eventually take him home to England when they left the country.

Another time, I was away on the other side of the country on business and Sue telephoned one evening.

"Guess what?" she said.

"You've acquired a dog," I replied immediately.

Sometimes you just know what's going to happen, don't you? She was amazed that I had guessed. Sue had flown back into Riyadh from the UK the night before and on the way from the airport quite close to our house she had seen a dog on the street.

Our new-found dog and yours truly

"Stop the car," she said to our friend who had picked her up from the airport. No sooner had she opened the car door than in jumped the dog, settled down and appeared completely at home. It moved right in to our house as though it had been there forever. For all the reasons we had previously agreed not to have pets, we realised we could not keep the dog and we started looking for a new home for our temporary adoptee.

However, it took a good few weeks to find it a good home. During this time we took it for walks in the desert and realised how much we missed the companionship and joy that a dog can bring to a home.

Yes, that is a river in the picture! It was purified waste-water and was clean enough to support goldfish and other life and was the main source of water for the packs of "desert dogs" roaming around the edges of the city. A little further down-stream the water just disappeared into a hole in the desert.

We turned down many potential owners for our foundling, some of whom obviously wanted the dog to use as a guard and others who looked as though they could not afford to feed themselves, let alone a growing dog. Eventually a prosperous looking couple arrived and the dog went straight to them with the sort of acceptance that dogs have for people they know they can trust. Dogs know these things.

We said they could have our new friend and they asked about what kind of food she ate, should they buy a bed, how long her lead should be. It was obvious that they had never owned a dog before but we felt she would have a good life with them. They could not take the dog for another two weeks, so her stay with us continued and we gave her the name Lucy that her new owners had chosen.

Later they returned with a new bed, collar, lead and cans of dog food, which they proudly showed us as proof of their good intentions. Sadly, we reluctantly handed Lucy over to start her new life but at least we were happy to know that we had probably saved her from starvation or from death on the roads. It was not unknown for some locals to drive directly at stray dogs. Such was their contempt for the animals.

Having said that we did not want pets whilst in Saudi, we were adopted by various cats during our unexpectedly long six and a half year stay. In our first house two white kittens appeared in our compound and declared that they had come to stay. We think that they had been thrown over the wall. One kitten had one green eye, the other blue. Eye, that is. Both kittens did have two eyes! Deaf as a post, the blue/green eyed kitten, as I believe such cats often are.

One green eye, one blue!

Much later on they moved house with us and both freaked out in their new surroundings. One ran away and we never saw it again and the other did not settle down in her new environment with our other cats. The same friends to whom we had given the "Labrador" puppy took her in, much to our relief.

There were stray cats everywhere in Riyadh. How they thrived, we'll never know but I suppose there were enough rubbish tips outside hotels, restaurants and houses among which they could forage for sufficient food. Water was not a problem, even in high summer as there were always sprinklers which watered the many gardens and parks.

In a small "compound" just across the road from our first house was a brick built electrical sub-station with a gap of about four inches under the steel door. It was the ideal place for cats to have their kittens in comfort and safety. From time to time we would see a line of tiny heads peering out at the big wide world from under the door and then the kittens would be gone to seek their fortune elsewhere once they no longer needed their mother's care. On one occasion I opened our compound door and before I could close it, seven tiny kittens rushed between my legs to take up residence with us. They must have seen that several other cats visited us from time to time and word must have gone around the cat world that we were an "easy" touch. The maximum number of cats we ever had living in the house was four but at times were probably feeding upwards of twenty at a time!

To ease the overpopulation problem and to avoid having to look for homes for potential offspring, we had decided early on that our two white female cats should be neutered. However, finding a vet in Riyadh was not easy, as there were none commercially in practice, i.e. open to the public. Eventually, we learned of a veterinary surgeon, whose husband, also a vet, was medical advisor to the stud farm and stables belonging to the King of Saudi Arabia - nice job! She ran an unofficial surgery in their third floor apartment. Sue made an appointment and took the first of our cats to have the operation. The surgery was in a small bathroom, clean but basic. Before starting the operation the vet called her 11-year old daughter in to assist.

"I'm busy," she said a little cheekily, so the vet asked Sue whether she'd mind holding the necessary instruments while she did the precision stuff. Sue didn't mind (I'm not sure whether I would have) and the operation passed off successfully.

On the way out Sue nearly stepped on a hedgehog and was advised that they had had the animal living happily in the apartment for some time. Apparently it frequently became lost under sofas and behind piles of books and they had to be a little careful wandering around with no shoes on, particularly at night.

Come the day when the second cat's turn came around the vet recognised Sue and said, "You're the one who doesn't mind blood and gore," and pressed her into service once more. We didn't get a rebate on her fee, however.

We did own one cat for over four years and it was with some sadness that we left "Kipper" behind with a German friend when we left. He was another "turn up" and we never found out where he came from. One night he simply appeared outside our gates and we left him some food and water. The next morning he was still there and he just ambled in and never left. Sue went home during part of the first Gulf War and I always made sure that Kipper was in the house with me at nights. I would take him into my makeshift shelter during air raids along with the radio, nuclear, biological and chemical protective suit and respirator, torch, gin and tonic (yes, gin and tonic) and other essential things one needs to survive scud missile attacks.

Kipper was more a dog than a cat and quite happily moved house with us four times. He would follow us to the tennis court and faithfully sit while we played, following the ball with his eyes as it went from end to end. At the swimming pool he would sit under our chairs and walk the pool by our side as we swam up and down. He met us at the door when we came home and we reckon he would have barked if he could, he was so dog like. We never took him into the desert but I'm sure he would have enjoyed it, just as much as did the dogs.

One of our diplomatic staff friends had the largest Yorkshire terrier in the world called Fred and a cat named Lucky, both of which we looked after occasionally. At the end of their stay in Riyadh the family moved to Greece and we cared for the animals while their owners came back to England prior to taking up their posts in Athens. We then arranged to ship their pets by air from Saudi Arabia to Greece. A daunting task in its own right, having to deal with various ministries and officials to get the paperwork right allowing them to be exported from the one country and imported to the other.

On the night they were due to travel we lightly fed them, dosed them with the prescribed tranquilisers, put them in their respective sky kennels and took them to the airport. It was one of those nights that felt like you were standing next to a hairdryer. Well over one hundred degrees and windy. We eventually found the freight depot and introduced our charges to an airport employee. He did not speak English and my Arabic was limited to, "good morning, how are you?" "go away" – very useful on occasion - and very little else. However, everything seemed in order and the animals were accepted for their long flight to Greece. We were assured that they would be kept in air-conditioned accommodation until just before boarding and not with the rest of the freight melting on the tarmac, so we left them to enjoy their trip.

Lucky was OK on arrival but our friends later told us that Fred was not quite as good a traveller. Somewhere along the way he decided he could not wait to get to the bathroom and let everything go in his cage. He was almost unrecognisable on arrival having rolled, sat or slept in his bathroom and only the smell was worse than his appearance. Apparently it made for a swift unhindered passage through immigration and customs though, so it wasn't all bad and after a thorough bath and disinfectant session, Fred seemed no worse for his experience. I don't know about their car though!

As you might imagine, our social life in Saudi Arabia was a little different to that which we had enjoyed in most other countries. Trips to the desert helped as did golf, tennis and swimming but we were also able to hold dinner parties and barbecues within our own communities, taking care to observe the strict local laws. On one such evening one of our guests stayed the night at our place as the party finished late and he had to start work extremely early in the morning. Before retiring for the night we said, "Just help yourself to breakfast before you go, you'll find everything you need in the kitchen cabinets and the fridge."

When we came down in the morning we were surprised to see a coffee cup, an empty cereal bowl and a half-empty carton of dry cat food on the kitchen counter top. It was pretty obvious to us that our guest had mistakenly eaten a generous helping of Brekkies (for cats) which just happened to also be in one of our kitchen cabinets, close to the cereals. He denied it of course, and still does to this day but we still smile when we think of him tucking in to the cat food on that morning after the night before. I suppose the copious quantity of "grape juice" consumed during the previous evening must have had something to do with his judgment so early the next morning. He seemed none the worse for it.

Nothing to do with dogs or cats but I must relate a tale that happened to some of my UK colleagues during a business trip to Saudi. They had flown into Dhahran on the Gulf Coast, finished their business there and decided to take the train to Riyadh instead of flying. Now, Dhahran railway station is a palatial edifice, marble halls, vaulted ceilings, and a large number of platforms. There were as many as two trains a day arriving and departing!

My friends had made their reservations, presented their tickets, shown their authority to travel and passed through the security gate similar to those with which we have become accustomed at airports. They boarded the train looking forward to relaxing, albeit alcohol free, on the daytime journey across the desert to the capital. All went well for a while, the train ran smoothly and their first class compartment was comfortable, if not luxurious.

After several hours travelling sedately across the desert, they felt a series of jolts and the train shuddered to a halt in the middle of nowhere. They knew from the rate of deceleration that the driver had obviously applied the brakes due to an emergency of some kind. There was much craning of necks out of the windows to see what was up and shortly the guard ran past them from the rear of the train heading for the engine.

It transpired from all the consternation that the train had struck several camels and there was a heated debate in progress about what was to be done.

Now, in earlier days the King of Saudi Arabia had decreed that if camels were killed by trains crossing the desert, the railway company would compensate the owner with a handsome cash payment. The camel was, and still is, a considerable asset in the harsh environs of the Arabian Desert and a man's wealth was calculated by the size of his herd.

The Bedouin are a canny lot as far as preserving the little they have. So it soon became their occasional practice to wheedle out the oldest, scrawniest and least valuable camels from their herds and, accidentally, of course, to graze them alongside the railway track. However, that law was changed and now it was no longer standard procedure that owners were recompensed for every camel that suffered collision with the trains.

Such was the case in this instance. The driver and guard were arguing hammer and tongs with the camel herder. Eventually, the train crew having apparently won their case, the train slowly moved off and gathered speed to resume its journey.

The guard returned to the rear of the train and all was well, at least, for a little while.

They had not travelled far when a couple of battered pick-up trucks came into view running alongside the train, clouds of dust billowing in their wake. Aboard were several irate Arabs wielding rifles and they were obviously not merely putting on a show for the passengers. Gradually, the trucks overtook the train and it was not much later that once again, the train shuddered to a screeching halt.

Once more the guard passed our friends on his way to the front of the train, this time with a little more haste and suitably armed, accompanied by a policeman who happened to be on board. The train having stopped on a curve, our friends could see that a pick-up truck had been positioned across the track and the driver had only just managed to stop the train in time. There was much shouting, brandishing of weapons and gesticulating and it was some time before peace was restored.

Fortunately no shots were fired and the outcome of the incident was that the driver of the pick-up truck was given a free ride to the capital, Riyadh, where no doubt he spent some time explaining his case to the local constabulary.

Such an incident was typical of the mixture of the old and the new cultures in Saudi Arabia.

Looking back on our time in the Arabian Desert, it was an experience we would not have missed for the world but after six and a half years we were ready to return to cooler, greener climes and our families.

Chapter Three

The First "Job"

Having decided not to pursue further employment, unless anything really interesting came along, our first house sitting "job" back home was in East Sussex during a fine spell of September weather looking after two small dogs, Daisy and Pooch. Their regular dog sitting people had let them down and, as I mentioned earlier, my sister had suggested that Sue and I might be happy to fill the gap. The dogs and their owner lived in an original Sussex stone built farmhouse on Ashdown Forest with a glorious southerly view. A nearby spring-fed pond led to adjacent fields, mixed woodland and a heath land golf course far across the valley below. The well-tended garden consisted of a series of terraced lawns and flowerbeds sloping down from the house towards a small orchard and then the fields.

A reed-lined pond, surrounded by majestic trees, contained a number of ghost carp that attracted a foraging heron most mornings. Fortunately, the edges of the pond had been netted so the heron was always unsuccessful in its quest for a meal and had to hunt elsewhere for his breakfast. We often sat in the garden watching the sun set over the valley and we can clearly remember the peace and quiet of those warm, late summer evenings as the mist would start to climb the valley towards us. If this was what house and pet sitting was all about we thought we could just about manage it.

On most evenings a number of deer, including a fine black doe, would emerge from the mist, come right up to the garden fence and eat fallen pears from the trees just in front of us. They were oblivious to our presence and only disappeared as darkness fell, merging the trees with the sky. Their presence was then only evident through the sounds of their nocturnal feasting.

One evening at twilight we were walking the dogs in fields not far from the house when we were startled to hear unusual noises from the other side of a high hedge. They sounded suspiciously like heavy and very deliberate footsteps keeping pace with us. We turned around at the bottom of the field and retraced our steps, then suddenly realised the footsteps had also turned and were still shadowing us. The dogs seemed unconcerned.

Eventually we came to a gap in the hedge and we were able to peer through the gathering gloom, only to come, startlingly, face to face with the beak and huge round eyes of an ostrich. Hardly what you'd expect in the heart of the English countryside. We don't know who was more frightened!

The next day we learned that there was an ostrich farm not too far away and our acquaintance of the previous evening was only one of many such birds down on the farm. This was during the period when ostrich farms such as this were springing up all around the country and many people were convinced that this was the latest "gold rush". A large number of people, including one of our friends, lost everything. We hope that this particular farm survived.

During that first stay we wondered whether we would be able to secure enough clients in the future to keep us occupied and, perhaps more importantly, to uphold the wisdom of our decision not to have pets of our own. We did not know then, that very soon we would be in danger of having too many bookings and be in the unfortunate position of having to turn people down.

We always took our own food and drink and, of course, the portable barbecue for each of our visits. Three years in the States and subsequent time spent in the deserts of Saudi

Arabia had served as a pretty thorough apprenticeship in the art of cooking on the grill. Even with the temperature in St. Louis at minus fifteen degrees Fahrenheit (they don't understand Centigrade in the US) we used to barbecue all kinds of meat – and vegetables. Roasts and even the Christmas turkeys were prepared over indirect heat on our Weber kettle charcoal grill. Fish and vegetables too tasted much better when cooked in the open air, particularly if the weather was kind enough to allow dining al fresco as well. We still get some pretty odd looks from neighbours when we barbecue in December at our present home base in Harrogate in North Yorkshire.

I digress. Our charges presented us with no problems during our stay but introduced us to a future client, in a roundabout way. We were out early one morning on one of those days when the dew lay like frost on the grass. Although it was still late summer, the morning air was cool enough to "illuminate" one's breath. Tiny spiders' webs clung to the grass and caught the sunlight, looking for all the world like thousands of small silver Bedouin tents stretching as far as the eye could see.

Climbing one of the many forest paths we walked through the trees which were just starting to show the tell tale changes in colour of autumn. We emerged at the top to look down on the heather lined fairways of one of the two golf courses which covered that side of Ashdown Forest. As they were built on common land, both courses were accessible to the public and were ideal for dog walking. Whilst we were walking down the side of one of the fairways a large male golden retriever loped up to us in a friendly fashion and seemed intent on joining us on our walk. Which is exactly what he did.

His owner was nowhere to be seen and he followed us around the golf course and all the way "home". I should tell you that our dogs' owner had mentioned that Daisy had just come out of season, so we had readily guessed the reason for the retriever's attentions. We locked our two dogs in the house, under protest I must add, as it seemed they wanted to play with their new-found friend. With the retriever on a lead, we then set off back to the golf course to the point where he had joined us. After many attempts to get him to leave us, he finally took off at great speed across the golf course in the opposite direction to our way home. Thankfully, we assumed he had scented his owner and that that would be the last we would see of him.

We were just a little surprised, therefore, to find him waiting expectantly at our gate when we returned. He had beaten us home, although he had not passed us on the way! Fortunately, his collar carried a disc with his owner's address and telephone number. We were therefore able to leave a message on an answer phone and resigned ourselves to hosting him until we heard, hopefully, from his owner. A good few hours later the owner, who had been playing golf that morning, called and arranged to meet us at a nearby popular pub.

Pagan

We sat in the traditional pub garden enjoying a well-earned drink in the late afternoon sunshine whilst we waited and were eventually rewarded by a joyful reunion between the dog and its grateful owner. We explained how we had found Pagan, the retriever, and why we were in the locality. We did not know then but it turned out some time later that Pagan and his friend Gunner, a German pointer, were to become regular wards of ours.

Our two week stay came to an end all too quickly and we left our first house sit not knowing what lay ahead in the shape of future commitments, or of the interesting times and immense enjoyment that was to follow over the next few years.

Chapter Four

The Rottweiler

Our first contact with prospective clients was normally through recommendation from friends, relatives or existing clients and many new clients would become friends of ours.

Some of our "jobs" were only for a few days, if there was not much travel involved, but others were for as long as five weeks. One such long stay was in Kent and it was with some apprehension that we went for our initial "interview" one Sunday lunchtime. Not so much that these were new clients, but they had not had anyone, other than family, look after their home before and one of their dogs was a Rottweiler!

"Come for lunch," they had said. "See how you get on with the dogs. If Olly, the rotty, approaches you, ignore her, don't come too close to us, don't go near her bed, etc, etc." More or less, "whatever you are going to do, don't do it."

The day arrived for our get-together and armed with the map they had faxed to us, we eventually turned off the last piece of public tarmac road and started up their long private lane. We passed a few typical brick and tile hung Kentish houses and one large Manor House behind its walled boundary, and at last bumped onto a grass centred track, for the last mile of the journey. Rabbits scattered off the track as we passed a marsh and a lake, and in the distance the house appeared set into the hillside at the head of a small valley.

Climbing the gradually sloping drive, we approached a five-barred gate and stopped. Searching for the bell hidden by creeper, in the distance above us we could see the dogs awaiting our arrival on the terrace of the house. The gate swung open automatically and we made our way to our meeting.

You might understand that we were more than a little apprehensive as we approached the house, especially when this huge dog looked down through the car window at us as we pulled to a stop.

Remembering the words of warning, we got out of the car as though nothing was amiss, did not shake hands with our hosts and generally smiled through chattering teeth hoping to appear completely unafraid of the big brown eyes watching our every move. We were invited into the house, followed closely by the dogs. Lunch started with gin and tonics, or is it gins and tonic? Who cares? This was followed by a full three-course meal, plenty of wine and much conversation as though we had all known each other for life. We had only expected a sandwich!

We took a walk round the garden, with the dogs of course, through the grounds and the surrounding fields. In one of their loose boxes they were nursing a young deer back to health. Their gardener had found it some days before, unable to stand unaided but with no apparent injury and the poor thing was still not able to get to its feet. As attempts to cure it had not proved successful they had telephoned a deer sanctuary, which was due to pick up the unfortunate animal the next day.

Sue was given a tour round the house by our lady owner whilst I was shown the technical bits of the building, burglar alarm, fuse boxes; that sort of thing. As Sue came down the stairs, she was greeted by Olly jumping up and putting her front paws on her shoulders. In a friendly way, of course. By then, we think Olly had sensed that we were not about to steal the silver or were a threat to her owners. A little later, as we left, we felt reasonably confident that we could go solo with Olly in a few weeks time. We just hoped that Rottweilers had good memories!

By the time we were due back at Olly's we had been asked to look after my sister's house and dogs about ten miles away for part of the time during our stay. Normally, we never liked to take on double bookings but we felt that we could not let either my sister or our new clients down. My sister's booking was for about the first week of our rotty "engagement" and it meant that I would be on my own with Olly for at least that week! As Sue would travel over each evening to prepare and share dinner with me, at least I would not starve.

Come the day, Sue and I arrived twenty four hours early to stay the night and "consolidate our relationship with Olly", before her owners and Sue left the next morning for their respective destinations. Sue, for just a few miles down the road and our hosts to Australia!

Early the next morning, I watched them all wend their way down the lane, Sue in our car and Olly's folks in a taxi bound for Heathrow. We were alone at last! Just me, Olly, Poppy the spaniel, a number of chickens, doves, trout, and an ailing twenty six year-old pony called Nibbs. As the owners were to be away for five weeks we had instructions on what to do if the pony did not survive their absence! Thankfully, digging was not on the list.

Nibbs had been the childrens' pony and had been retired for some years as the "children" were by now in their mid-twenties. The pony had been loved so much by all the family that they just could not bear to part with him, as they were such caring people and, even at his ripe old age, Nibbs was still enjoying his well earned retirement.

However, Olly was my main and immediate concern. I have to tell you that I tried not to stray too far from my mobile phone in case I needed to call for the vet, the RSPCA or the cavalry if I became trapped upstairs, or anywhere, by the seventy or eighty pounds of muscle on four legs with huge teeth! Olly's party trick, well one of them, was to wait until I went upstairs and then refuse to let me down by standing at the bottom of the stairs growling menacingly! Fortunately I devised a cunning plan, which worked every time. The house had a staircase at both ends and they were linked through the bedrooms. I was therefore able to get down the other staircase and meet Olly on the same level as though I had never been upstairs. She fell for it every time.

Darkness fell on my first day. All the animals, birds and fish had been fed and watered, well, not the fish, and I settled down on the sofa in front of the TV for a peaceful evening. Before long Olly approached and stared at me with her big brown eyes. She looked ominous, her eyes reflecting the flickering light from the TV and the table lamps. This was her territory and I was a stranger. What next?

She growled softly and very slowly put one paw on my knee. She sat like that for a while looking directly into my face and then the other front paw came up to join the first. What can you say to such a dog?

"Good girl Olly," seemed useless but I said it anyway and achieved no response.

"Lie down," in my most commanding voice had no effect either. My mobile phone, just when I needed it most, was in my coat pocket three rooms away. It might as well have been on the moon!

Still growling, she moved again and suddenly she was completely in my lap, her nose and teeth about six inches from my face and only a tad or two more from my throat.

I could see the morning headlines. "Rottweiler traps man in armchair for a week."

I had heard the one about "What do you do when a Rottweiler is humping your leg?"

I didn't think that the answer, "Fake an orgasm," would be appropriate at that moment so I tried desperately to recall what the owners, Jane and Paul, had said that might get the dog's attention.

"Walkies," they had said was the sure-fire way to get Olly to do what you wanted her to do, i.e. to go for a walk or simply to distract her. I had thought at the time of our briefing that "walkies" might only be appropriate for a docile lap dog, or one of similar size and of a much more affable disposition. But, as my last resort, I tried it.

As nonchalantly as I could, under the circumstances (and the dog, you will recall) I confidently croaked "walkies" and, to my utter amazement, she slowly backed down off my knees, gently took my hand in her mouth and led me to the front door. I didn't actually want to go for a walk at that time but I really had no choice and there wasn't much on television anyway.

Previously, we had asked where Olly slept and her owners had kindly resisted responding with the old chestnut, "anywhere she likes". In fact, both she and Poppy slept in purpose-built wooden kennels, which were due for replacement in the near future, in a run under an open barn close to the house. That night I had little trouble getting the dogs into their run using the tried and tested method of biscuit diplomacy. Phew, I thought. This was not going to be so difficult after all.

All else was secure, the doors and windows were locked, burglar alarm set and so to bed. I had just drifted off to sleep when a huge crash outside summoned me back to near consciousness. The security lights had come on around the exterior of the house and as I peered out of the window, two great big brown eyes supported by the muscular shoulders of Olly were looking up at me from the driveway! She had escaped from her kennel and was now at large in the night!

Sleep was now out of the question for me, at least for a while. Dressed, and armed with the biggest torch I could find and the all-important biscuits, I ventured out into the night to do battle with the unknown. However, Olly quite readily followed me back to the kennel and seemed to say, "Didn't I do well?" She had burst right through the kennel wall. It brought back memories of Turner and Hooch or Beethoven (two good movies, if you haven't seen them), only this was real. The gaping hole in the side wall of her kennel told the story. It was fortunate that there was sufficient in the way of wooden planking and an old door in the barn for me to undertake a repair that would last all five weeks of my stay. Olly went back in like a lamb and we had no further nonsense that night.

Sooty, Megan & Olly

Some days after, whilst walking the dogs one afternoon we saw a huge fox in the fields at the back of the house. I was so pleased that Olly did not jump the fence to give chase. She could have cleared the fence with ease as she demonstrated on another walk by soaring over a double stile at least some four feet apart. Olly was also surprisingly tolerant towards sheep. Many times we walked through fields full of sheep and both Olly and Poppy acted as though they were not there.

Not so with rabbits! Poppy had a fine turn of speed and out-manoeuvred the rabbits with ease. On many occasions we had to prise rabbits from her jaws and very few survived the experience. Olly never caught any that she chased, which was just as well. Despite our improving relationship, I would not have attempted to retrieve a rabbit from her jaws.

We were very surprised to see so many black rabbits on the property and we later learned that they had been introduced to Britain during the Second World War for food, being easier to spot and therefore shoot than ordinary rabbits. Ambiguously, they were called sportsmen's rabbits.

Perhaps at this point a description of the property might help. There had been a well-documented dwelling on the site since the tenth century. That's pretty old in anyone's language! An old Roman road, (did you ever hear of a new one?) leading from the Sussex iron smeltings, ran nearby, so maybe people lived there in even earlier times. Those early settlers must have known a thing or two for it to have survived as a residential site over the years. They obviously realised that this was an ideal sheltered spot. Perhaps, because of the stream running through what must have then been a forest and with ample stone and wood nearby with which to build the first structure.

Imagine a long, timber framed house facing west, set into a bank which sloped down to a stream with ponds and dams allowing the stream to drop several feet from south to north as one looked away from the house. All manner of shrubs, rhododendrons, azaleas and vibernum, among others, clothed the banks forming a riot of colour, and mature trees framed the whole picture. A dovecote nestled among the shrubs on the other side of the stream on the far bank which rose up and away from the house. A cloud of white doves whirled in continuous motion above.

In the distance there was mature woodland and several small lakes, some of which contained trout. Nearby, forming part of the garden, was a small, long disused quarry which provided a superb backdrop for a fish pond, a waterfall, a rustic wooden bridge and many species of water loving plants, including the huge umbrella-shaped leaves of a gunnera. Trees and shrubs grew up and around the steep quarry walls. The whole setting formed an idyllic picture and a thoroughly delightful place for a house. Let no one say that our ancestors were not as astute as ourselves when it came to choosing sites for their dwellings!

In this bucolic environment wildlife prospered as it also probably had over the centuries. During our stay we had the opportunity to closely observe many different varieties. Often, a grass snake crossed the stream near the stepping-stones right in front of the house. Pied wagtails frequently courted on the drive and were building a nest in the creeper on the wall by the front door. Swallows were diving for flies over the stream and here we heard our first cuckoo of the year. There were goldfinches on the lawn and a blue tit landed on Sue's shoulder for several seconds whilst she was sitting quietly in the sunshine one evening. Often, sitting in peaceful silence by the stream we saw a kingfisher patrolling its territory, although we never found out where it nested.

On one beautiful afternoon with temperatures in the high 60s and clear blue skies, I emptied the rainwater out of a boat moored at a small jetty among the reeds on the trout lake and tried my hand at fly-fishing. Thankfully, the trout were not interested - particularly as I did not have a landing net with me. Most likely it was due to my lack of skill and the time of day.

After periods of several days without rain I had to clear a filter on an electric pump immersed in the stream below, switch on the pump and run a long hosepipe into the lakes to aerate the water in order for the trout to breathe.

Most evenings were warm enough to have a relaxing sundowner on the terrace outside and to fire up the ever-present barbecue. This sort of life certainly was a far cry from climbing aboard the crowded 7.35 am every day from Chelsfield, near Biggin Hill in Kent, to central London and returning in the late evening, or wearing a collar and tie in the heat of Riyadh.

During our stay we followed with interest the progress of a duck and her eight offspring, which took up residence on one of the many ponds in the stream in front of the house. We watched them struggle up the ramp from the stream on to a purpose-built island where they were safe from foxes and the dogs. Eventually, they learned to fly, mainly due to spaniel-assisted take-offs from the lawn. It was quite spectacular seeing them in formation on final approach making a rapid spiral descent through the trees and onto their extremely short liquid landing strip.

Various sets of parents and ducklings seemed to shuttle between the ponds and the lakes and the numbers also seemed to vary. Sometimes ducklings were left on their own at both locations and there would be crises of identity between which ducklings belonged in the same family and to which parents. Territorial squabbles were common! We never knew exactly how many drakes, ducks and ducklings there were but we guessed that the foxes had a hand in the equation and in the seemingly diminishing numbers somewhere along the line.

Two geese and their goslings appeared on the largest of the lakes. Occasionally, swans flew high overhead but they seldom visited us and we suspected that they were looking for larger stretches of water upon which to settle.

Also, one day we were surprised to see a colourful model duck floating on one of the lakes. His painted body of yellow, red, buff and navy blue was a detailed testament to a fine-brush painter's skill.

We were stunned when it suddenly paddled away to the other end of the lake and then took to the air. We rushed "home" to consult our ever-present bird book to find that it was a male Mandarin duck.

Smarty Pants

They are the showiest ducks you are ever likely to see and we saw "smarty pants" many times over the years but never with a lady friend of his own; only his Mallard friends.

One day, two baby doves fell, or were pushed, out of the dovecote into a huge rose bush directly underneath. One had died but we managed to catch the other and install it in a cardboard box on the warming plate beside the Aga. The next morning the dove was still alive but I was not sure if it was eating or drinking. We tried to get it to take water but regrettably the dove did not survive the next night. We rescued several more "dropouts" from the dovecote and subsequently achieved a pretty good survival rate by housing them in an empty loose box until they were strong enough to fly away to join the rest of their community.

On another fine day in the garden our friendly grass snake gave us an exhibition by swimming the whole length of the section of stream just opposite the door and rested its head on one of the dams.

Our peace was shattered one afternoon by a great crash, which sent us running down to the barns to see what had happened. Olly and Poppy had demolished a large, high stack of timber destined to become logs, in their search for, and eventual success in catching, a hapless rabbit hiding at the bottom of the pile.

Never let it be said that house sitting is dull. One late spring night I was enjoying the peace and quiet of the night sky, taking the dogs out for their last walk of the day while Sue took a relaxing bath. Apart from the occasional excitement when one of the dogs chased an unsuspecting rabbit there was little to disturb the tranquillity. I was about half a mile down the lane leading from the garden gate to the outside world when in the distance I heard the faint sound of a voice calling my name, Trevooooor, Trevor, TREVOR it wailed down the hitherto quiet country track. I stopped and listened and suddenly realised it was Sue and she sounded as though she needed my immediate attention, if not actual help. I raced back up the lane followed by the excited dogs in full cry, scattering the rabbits right and left, wondering what on earth I would find.

All I could see on approaching the house was Sue hanging out of the bedroom window, very inappropriately attired. I dashed into the house and up the stairs! As I reached the landing she was standing wrapped in a towel pointing wordlessly to a black shape flitting around the room.

It transpired that she had just immersed herself in the bath, grateful for the soothing warm scented water, when she had a feeling that something like a smooth shadow had flown through the bedroom doorway and into the bathroom. It flew silently round the space above the exposed wooden beams below the high pitched ceiling and appeared much bigger than an insect but smaller than a bird. It then landed on a beam and....... hung upside down!

She realised with a start, that it was a bat. Having never seen a bat that close before, she was fascinated but tried to forget all the old wives' tales of such creatures getting tangled in one's hair. Or worse still, scratching and having rabies, or even the older tales of vampires! The only real problem was she was stark naked, the bat was hanging at head height directly above her and the towel was on the rail over the end of the bath. This meant her having to stand up and crouch down to avoid the bat, and hope that it did not take off and that old wives' tales were just that, tales.

As Sue's initial shock subsided and changed to concern for the bat's safety rather than her own she decided the only thing she could do was to get out of the bath and summon help. She slowly stood, bent dripping under the beam and grabbed the towel. Throwing it around her, she dashed to the window and wailed into the night. At that point the bat followed her! She said later that it was wonderful to watch it fly around and around, so fast, but silently and without hitting anything. A bird in the same circumstances would have crashed into the walls and windows in its fright and confusion.

After I had broken the half mile record in getting back to the house, our initial joint attempts to get the bat out failed. We flapped our arms about, made imitation bat noises and generally made fools of ourselves, finally collapsing in laughter. Eventually, exhausted, we just turned out the lights, opened all the windows and we sat on the stairs in the quiet of the evening. As the evening breezes blew through the house, the black shadow silently found its own way out into the night sky.

During our five week stay Olly became quite attached to us. In fact, Olly and I watched the Monaco Grand Prix together one Sunday afternoon, interrupted as usual, by the inevitable "walkies!" to get her off my lap. On subsequent visits it was plain to see that she remembered us. Fortunately the old wooden kennels had been replaced with purpose built, roofed, metal cages with kennels inside and we did not have any more night escapes!

However, on one subsequent visit we did have a daytime breakout but not by Olly. We were sitting in the garden reading Bill Bryson's "Notes From a Small Island" one afternoon. I was reading passages aloud and we were falling about laughing at situations that we recognised, had been there and, in most cases, done that. The only difference between Bill and ourselves is that he has far more skill and expertise at recording his experiences than we ever will.

Our mirth was loudly interrupted by a great commotion at the gate at the end of the drive. Olly and the other dogs were having a verbal set to with two Labradors just the other side of the gate. Butch and Sundance were two of the largest male Labradors we have ever seen and they lived down the lane in a bungalow on Olly's owner's land about half a mile from the garden gate.

Ordinarily, they were confined to their house or garden whilst their owner, an American named Todd, who was "something in the city", was at work. Todd did not have to be in the office until lunch- time, to coincide with working hours on Wall Street on the other side of the "pond". Consequently, the dogs normally had a good run each morning and were quite used to being left alone during the afternoon and early evening. However, this particular afternoon they had escaped and we needed to do something about it.

We secured our dogs in the house, rounded up Butch and Sundance without too much of a problem as we all knew each other well and walked them back to their bungalow. A quick repair of the fence did the trick, or so we thought.

Peace was restored, we freed our dogs and we settled back down to continue reading about Bill Bryson's escapades. Only about twenty minutes had passed when there was a repeat performance of the altercation at the gate. Butch and Sundance were there again and this time they were soaking wet. It was pretty obvious that, as Labradors do, they had sought out the nearest body of water and had had a wonderful time. Not only were they wet but also they were black with mud, obviously from the edges of our owner's lakes, which were home to trout, ducks, moorhen and a variety of other wildlife. I use the word "were" in the previous sentence because, at the time, I feared the worst. I could picture the devastation these two dogs might have caused during their freedom.

We retraced our steps to their bungalow, hosed the dogs down, found a substantial roll of wire and made a more permanent repair of the fence.

We diverted on our way back to "our" house to survey the damage at the lakes. Reeds and water plants had been flattened and there were great slide marks where the dogs obviously had launched themselves into the water. There was not much wildlife to be seen. Any birds that might have been on the lake probably, and sensibly, had taken refuge in the undergrowth or flown away. However, there didn't appear to be any blood or feathers anywhere either so perhaps no real damage had been done after all.

We never really knew whether this was the case. At that time the ducks, and their ducklings were continually moving from ponds to lakes and back again so keeping count of the actual population was impossible. However, we did think that there were a few ducklings less after that day.

On another occasion, Butch and Sundance went AWOL again while we were looking after Olly but the first we knew of it was on an answer- phone message.

"I have your tenant's Labradors", the recording said but we were unable to catch the caller's name. Our only recourse was to traipse down the lane, passing the now all too familiar hole in the fence, and we started to knock on neighbours' doors to enquire about the two escapees. When I say neighbours I'm not talking about next door here. As we were in deepest rural Kent, next door could be a mile down the lane.

We tried several places, everything from huge country houses with wrought iron gates and dauntingly long tree-lined drives, to modest farm cottages with postage stamp sized front gardens. At last we found one elderly lady who, after we explained about the phone call, asked us what type of voice it was. We said it was a youngish male with a southern accent. She said, "Do you mean educated?"

This question rather stunned us. Particularly Sue, who hails originally from the North of England but does not have an identifiable accent. However, sadly, on reflection later, we realised that a great number of people living in the South of England do have a perception that northerners cannot be educated to the same degree as their southern counterparts. Mostly, it seems, because of the difference in accents.

This poses the eternal question. Where does the north begin? To most southerners, it might be Potter's Bar or the Watford Gap, just north of London. But to someone living in the north, it might mean Scotland. Who knows?

I'm always amused by the signs on the Great North Road (The A1) which proudly announce "The North" even as far north as the old Wetherby roundabout in Yorkshire. I guess it all depends where you start from!

Anyway, Sue said, to the afore mentioned elderly lady, "No, I mean a southern accent."

Then she said that it was probably one of the local farm managers and gave us a name and phone number. On contacting him he said he'd had the dogs all day and that they had had a great time "helping" him on the farm. We suspected that it was not the first time the pair had visited him and an hour or so later he turned up with the two culprits in the back of his venerable battered Land Rover. Dirty, tired and hungry, Butch and Sundance were glad to see us and more than happy to return home. We thought that it was good that there are still people out there that are willing to look after "runaways" rather than turn them away, or turn them in to the dog warden.

We looked after Butch and Sundance ourselves, occasionally, after that episode, sometimes on a "live-in" basis and sometimes just for the day. They were great dogs, full of energy and despite their size and boisterousness, very obedient.

We had seen many dogs enjoy rolling in snow or wet grass but Sundance often did something we had never seen done by other dogs. We were out walking with them off their leads in a field of wet grass when we came upon a long steep slope. Sundance ran forward, launched himself into the air landing on his side on the slippery grass and slid for several yards down the slope. It was obviously a deliberate act and he certainly enjoyed it. On coming to a halt he would get up, run back up the slope and repeat the experience. He would only stop when we had passed him, reached the bottom of the slope ourselves and called him to us.

Sadly, Butch and Sundance, together with their owner, who was over in England to make his fortune in Oil Futures, moved back to the USA. So, sadly, we no longer looked after them.

Whether he really made his fortune we do not know. However, we did keep in touch with Todd, and on a long road trip from Florida to Canada and back, we met up with them all again. Their new home is on the shores of Lake Ontario in New York State. So now not only did the dogs have their own pond in the garden, but also instant access to one of the largest lakes in the world.

Todd was renovating a delightful old house, which has a history dating back to the slave trade times. It was a ramshackle, rambling house with cellars and tunnels leading to the lake, which enabled the slaves to be hidden from the local authorities. He had taken on a mammoth task as the house was huge, with much timber that required replacement and acres of mature garden.

Todd told us that he had loved England and was sorry that business forced him to leave. He also said that the people were so pleasant to him and that the countryside was so lush and green. It was just a pity it didn't have a roof! We know what he meant! Britain does have one of the most benign climates in the world. Trouble is, the weather is so bad! In reality, we actually have less than half the annual rainfall experienced in Florida, for example. However, in the United Kingdom it comes down much less heavy, more frequently, for longer periods and, of course, it is much colder. Thankfully, however, we do not have Florida's almost unbearable summer humidity or the threat, from approximately June to October each year, of potentially devastating hurricanes.

As Todd allegedly had made a reasonable pile of money in England, or so the local girls thought, he was much in demand on his return to his small hometown. He told us that his first few nights in his local bar were so embarrassing as all the local mothers paraded their daughters in front of him as the most eligible bachelor in town. Added to his rumoured fortune, he had also bought the biggest house in town and he was no ugly duckling. It eventually became so bad that he now dated girls only from other towns.

Since Todd had deserted the noise of open-outcry trading in the financial world of the City of London he had ventured into pastures new, literally. He had started a business taking wealthy Americans to our premier horse racing meetings such as Ascot, The Grand National and The Derby. Horse racing had been a passion of his during his stay in England and we know he had the connections, the ability and the charm to make a great success of such an enterprise.

We like to think that Butch and Sundance remembered us on our visit but they were such friendly dogs that they probably gave every visitor the long lost friend welcome that they gave us. We met the rest of Todd's family at dinner that evening and stayed the night with Todd and the dogs. We then moved on the next day, glad that we had seen them all again but sad to think that we would most probably never pass that way again.

****

Coming back to these shores, on a subsequent, short notice, one-day visit to look after Olly, some months after our first visit, she recognised me straight away, and it was as though I had never been away. It was mid July and the garden was looking superb, much more full-grown and greener than during our previous long stay some fifteen months previously. Two new spaniels, Megan and a puppy called Sooty had joined the family making four dogs in all, and two cows had appeared on the scene.

Earlier that year Mandy, one of the daughters of the house had married a South African and the wedding reception had been held in a marquee on the lawns between the house and the stream. At the reception, the bridegroom, Mark, had explained during his speech that it was normal practice in his country to consult the local witch doctor to ascertain the bride price. So, Mark related, on a recent trip home to South Africa he had been to see the local wise man who had thrown the appropriate powders on the fire. There was a flash and the witch doctor sucked his teeth said, "mmmn not good".

Our bridegroom informed his audience that he had urged him to try again. This he did, with the same result. At the third try, presumably with more powder a good deal extra rattling of bones and maybe a little cash incentive, the shaman exclaimed that the omens were now good and that his bride was worth two good head of cattle.

At this point in his speech Mark strode across to the wall of the marquee, and with a flourish threw back the canvas and said, "Here they are". Sure enough, there were two fine ribbon bedecked Sussex Brown cattle standing on the lawn contentedly chewing the cud.

Back to our short visit, the weather was glorious, sometimes eighty degrees and daylong sunshine. Many times I thought about how relaxing it was not to have to suffer the daily grind to work and back.

Meanwhile, back in my "office" on the terrace, earlier that day I had started the Daily Telegraph crossword and by now had it half completed when I went inside for a moment to answer the telephone. I left the newspaper on the terrace floor by my chair. Big mistake, as when I returned only a few minutes later Sooty had finished the crossword... along with the rest of the back page of the paper which was now in tatters spread across the lawn.

Ah well, there was always the view. I sat back and took it all in. Two of the many white doves strutted in line astern across the lawn to the edge of the stream, engaged in some kind of courting ritual of which only they were aware. Peace, the humming of bees, the relaxing sound of cooing doves and the plaintive bleating of far away sheep, as though they had lost their mothers. Maybe they had.

As melodious birdsong echoed across the small valley in front of me, only the raucous crows occasionally made their presence felt as an acceptable interruption to the early evening soundscape. Even the dogs too, were satisfied enough at this time of the day not to give chase to a foolhardy rabbit that appeared just across the stream, obviously unaware of our presence.

The sun was on its way down but still high in the western sky. I imagined a static horticultural fireworks display in front of me across the lawn towards the stream and rising up the opposite bank. At the water's edge, tall stalks of silver comet ornamental grass rose into their white plumes from an explosion at their bases formed by slender green leaves bursting upwards and outwards to all points of the compass. A light bright green conifer provided a permanent Roman candle some ten feet high. A much taller birch tree thrust its silver trunk to the sky with the leaves shimmering in the setting sun. A clump of foxgloves, some more than eight feet tall with their flowers just about spent, except at the very top, looked like purple rockets with long green exhaust trails.

Amazing what you can see on a lazy summer's afternoon when you've all the time in the world and the only pressing decision is whether to have a cold beer or a chilled glass of white wine before dinner.

****

The years passed by, during which we visited this idyllic setting at least annually, and Olly inevitably grew older and more infirm. It was time to think of a replacement for the time when poor old Olly could no longer take on the role of intruder deterrence. A Rottweiler puppy was the answer and subsequently, two, not one were purchased and introduced to the family.

By this time Mandy and Mark had moved to South Africa. Grandchildren were now on the scene and the family thought that a rotty puppy would be the ideal burglar alarm/deterrent for their offspring in foreign climes. So, one time we came to stay there were now three spaniels, one mature Rottweiler and two puppies. I say puppies reservedly because, of course, even at only nine weeks old they were actually bigger than the spaniels. Chobé was the one destined to replace Olly, and Scoobie had been named by the grandchildren as the one bound for Africa. It should really have been the other way round. I hadn't heard the name Chobé much since I was fortunate enough back in the 60s to stay at the Chobé Safari Lodge in Botswana.

Scoobie & Chobé, or is it Chobé & Scoobie?

There's another story there, but another time.

Scoobie and Chobé were great fun, but hard work. Fortunately they did not sleep in the house as they had been allocated a loosebox and horse yard in which they were to spend much of their time. They kept each other amused and raced around with the spaniels. Olly, of course, being top dog often had to put them in their place with ferocious growls and the odd snap. However, there was never any real threat to either puppy, even when one of them would somehow get its head right inside Olly's mouth.

We must have got through reams and reams of newspaper during our stay coping with the nasty end of puppy care. Better in the loosebox than in the kitchen though and it didn't really seem too much of a chore each morning compared with the fun of having two huge, boisterous puppies around.

We had one scary moment with them. The horse yard had been made puppy proof by the use of chicken wire, planks of wood, etc and every space through which it was expected a puppy could squeeze had been blocked with something or other. We would customarily put the puppies in their "run" whenever we were on our way out for a while or when we were walking the other dogs. The run was out of sight of the house but within earshot. It was usual to hear some yapping when the puppies had been locked in but this normally soon stopped.

I had just put the puppies in and returned to the house when I heard a yelping, which did not stop. My immediate reaction was that one of them had somehow injured itself. I raced down to the yard and saw the cause of the problem straight away. Chobé had somehow managed to wedge her head between the edge of the stable and a steel gatepost, reminiscent of the small boy with its head stuck in the railings story.

I just could not see how she had managed to do it as the gap seemed large enough only for her neck. She was in great distress by this time and I could not readily see how to free her. Crowbars and hacksaws, even the fire brigade, flashed through my mind but I had no time to reach any of those. Chobé was frothing at the mouth and she was clearly very upset. I attempted gently to push her backwards, turning her head to find the narrowest point in her skull, but to no avail. I then tried to reason which way to force her head back through the gap, which might cause her the least damage. I could see me later explaining to her owners, "Sorry about the fractured skull but she is still alive and the gate isn't damaged at all!"

This all sounds quite a tranquil situation whilst putting it down on paper but you might care to remember that I had a distraught, noisy puppy on my hands and I needed to take some pretty quick, positive action. Scoobie didn't help the situation either, as she was joining in the action and I couldn't get in to remove her from the scene, as I would not have been able to open the gate without crushing Chobé. As you might imagine, by this time, I'm also not my usual cool, calm, collected self either. At least you could reason with a child and explain that it would only be at matter of time before the fire brigade arrived with cutting equipment.

I figured that it might be better to break her jaw rather than her skull so I placed one hand on the top of her head just above her eyes, grasped the gatepost, closed my eyes and steadily increased pressure. Nothing happened, so I had to increase the force. Suddenly, without the cracking sound I feared as if something had broken, there was a yelp of pain, a sudden movement and she had popped out the other side.

Chobé calmed down more quickly than I did! By this time I was a trembling wreck. A couple of dog biscuits and a cup of strong tea soon sorted us both out and life returned to normal.

****

By the time we next visited the house, Scoobie had departed for her life in the sunshine. Cape Town sounded a much better bet for her, having three young children to play with and all those glorious beaches upon which to frolic. Given the choice between there and the soggy fields of Kent in winter, I know where I'd rather be!

Chobé was by now as big as Olly and still growing at less than a year old. We were there for the whole month of February whilst our owners went over to visit Scoobie and, more importantly, by now, the grandchildren.

Easy, I thought, by now Chobé would be housetrained and much easier to handle. I got on so well with all the other dogs, including Olly, that I envisioned an easy time in front of the log fire catching up with correspondence and bringing up to date all those things on my computer that I wouldn't need to do if I didn't have one. If you see what I mean!

Dog sitting is usually a relaxing, rewarding task combining moderate exercise, comfortable living, plenty to do and the companionship gained from faithful, friendly affectionate dogs. However, two things we have learned that we should try to avoid are puppies and sick dogs. Puppies are a huge amount of extra work and responsibility and you just can't relax, especially if you are on your own and you are always concerned that they might disappear or befall some dreadful accident.

Sick dogs, of course, are also always more of a burden and there was always the additional worry that things might get worse and we might be held, albeit maybe not openly, responsible for the ailing dog's worsening health. Old Ben, who features in the next chapter, was a potential case in point as you will see.

Just two days before arriving to look after Olly and company we received an e-mail from Jane and Paul saying that she had had part of one of her toes removed and would require extra care.

"Would that be all right?" They asked.

Of course, we couldn't say no, but we knew that we'd be having a difficult month with Olly. Sure enough, when we arrived we learned that Olly's right rear foot was heavily bandaged and that she could not be let out without first placing a plastic bag over the dressing.

Easy, yes? No. Far from it.

Jane showed us how easy it was to slip the bag over Olly's foot and tie a bow in the piece of bandage, which had been threaded through holes at the top of the bag. Olly tolerated the procedure with only a little growl. There was a muzzle available if things got too scary! She had had the operation on Friday, this was Sunday and we had to take her to the vet on Monday morning. We were advised that the foot had to be covered each time Olly went outside to prevent the bandage and thereby the wound from getting wet.

Our owners left. They were obviously most concerned and had even seriously thought of cancelling the trip due to Olly's predicament. Or was it ours?

The time came for Olly to do what we all have to do from time to time and we faced the prospect of the plastic bag routine. I have to add that it wasn't a huge bag, as in a supermarket shopping bag or anything like that, but actually a three by eight inch saline drip bag donated by the vet.

As soon as I lifted Olly's leg I knew that I was going to have trouble. There was the low growl, the feigned (I hoped) snap of the jaws and the convulsive removal of her leg from my grasp. "Oh shit!" I thought, "Why am I doing this?"

It wasn't like this was going to be a one off experience. We knew that we'd have to do this at least four times a day until her foot healed and that there would be several trips to the vet involved. The muzzle was our salvation. It was a single piece of nylon material shaped like a funnel, which slipped over the business end of the head with straps that came up under her throat and clipped together at the back of her neck. It was quite good really, as with a bit of practice I could creep up, slip it over her muzzle before she realised what was happening and only have to cope with mild dissention as I clipped the ends together.

However, the first time didn't quite work like that. Olly seemed very aware of what was coming and twisted herself out of my way before I could get the thing in place. It took me several attempts to get the muzzle on and, of course, by that time both of us were hot under the collar. It was then relatively easy to slip the bag over her dressing, holding her leg in one hand and the bag in the other. However, when releasing her leg to tie the bandage, using both hands, she swiftly withdrew her foot and off popped the bag. Back to square one! I only solved the problem by jamming my foot behind her leg to prevent it moving after I had let go. Once the bag was securely tied, tight, I had been told, to avoid it coming off whilst outside, I used a bit of biscuit diplomacy hoping that she would get used to it and only remember the treat and not the pain involved.

Phew, task achieved, only several tens more times before I didn't need to perform it any more. Of course, the whole procedure had to be reversed on the way back in.

Monday morning arrived and I wasn't looking forward to our trip to the vet's. It was bad enough getting the bag on board, never mind getting Olly in and out of the car, into the vet's and up on to the table. In the event, it wasn't too traumatic. By now I'd had a few practices of the bag on the foot routine and Olly jumped in the back of the Range Rover as though we were off on a pleasure jaunt. She didn't want to jump out at the other end, bearing in mind that the tailgate was quite a height from the ground, her bad foot and that Olly was no Spring chicken. However, with the aid of her lead and the inevitable biscuit she got down without injury and I led her into the vet's. I had, of course checked out that the coast was clear in the waiting room as I didn't want her to eat any little old ladies or their little dogs!

Once inside, the muzzle went on again and it was then that I learned that it was my job to lift her on to the table and hold her down whilst the vet did whatever she needed to do. Olly wasn't as heavy as I had feared and in no time at all, with some struggling and growling on her part and a bit of effort on mine, it was all done. Thank heavens for the muzzle; she would have required an injection without it. Down from the table, muzzle off, biscuit administered and we were back in the car and heading home. I think the vet thought I was more concerned than the dog as she gave me some pills for Olly to take to quieten her down prior to her next visit.

That was Monday. For the next Friday's vet appointment at ten in the morning I duly gave Olly two of the little white pills two hours before her trip to the vet. They didn't seem to make a great difference although she was just a little bit quieter and didn't seem to struggle as much as on her previous visit. The vet was pleased with her progress but the bandage and plastic bag were still required to protect her wound so I resigned myself for a busy time ahead.

I'd had to ask the vet for another plastic bag as the first one was in bad shape, literally. The holes had burst and the strip of bandage was covered in mud, frayed, and could not easily be secured and untied. Whilst at the vet's I saw another dog with a very smart bootie, silver leather with a non-slip sole and a lace up front – just like a shoe.

"Where can I get one of those which will fit Olly?" I asked.

I was advised that they could get me one in time for our next visit. I quickly made an executive decision and ordered one on behalf of Olly and her owners.

Back from the vet's, the day wore on and Olly grew more and more listless. A bonus for me but I was getting worried that she didn't want to go out, eat or drink. She tried to stand up, slipped on the stone floor and fell over!

It seemed like a good time to phone the vet, which I did. I explained the situation and as both the people I'd seen that morning were not there they said they'd get back to me. Some time later, I was reassured by the vet that this was a normal reaction from the little white pills! Only the timing was a little off. "She should be out for about twenty four hours," they said.

Memo to me: Give Olly the pills a little earlier next time! I never thought that two tiny pills could have such an effect on such a hefty dog.

Olly's food had been halved during this time, which was just as well. She was getting more than her normal share of biscuits.

I took delivery of Olly's new boot on the next visit to the vet's. What a difference that made. I was happier fitting it and taking it off, although I still used the muzzle. Olly was much more comfortable as it didn't flap around or make any noise when she walked and she grew quite used to it. Her foot was better protected, the boot stayed on whilst the plastic bags had slipped off once or twice, and she could now run with the other dogs.

Of course, during the whole time Olly was incapacitated the weather did not cooperate one bit. It was February after all. It rained and rained for the first two weeks, not too pleasant with five dogs to feed, exercise and tidy up after without having the extra hassle with keeping Olly's foot clean and dry. Olly, at this stage, normally slept outside with her cage door open so that she could roam the grounds at night. Whilst she was bandaged I was to keep her door closed at night to protect her foot. This was too much for both Olly and me as it meant the muzzle and boot routine just to get her to her kennel, some fifty yards or so from the house.

Olly and I agreed on a much better plan. I would let her sleep in the kitchen if she would keep quiet all night. Often the dogs would bark at night, probably because they had scented a fox or deer or a rabbit had dared to enter their territory, far enough away in their kennels not to be too troublesome a noise.

Unfortunately, Olly did not keep to her side of the bargain. On more than one occasion in the dead of night she picked up on the other dog's barking and joined in, in spades. She would start off with a normal bark and then it would develop into a howl. As my bedroom was not far removed, directly above the kitchen I could hear every decibel. Again, more than once, I got up, got dressed, down stairs, muzzle on, bootie on, door open, only to see Olly take one sniff of the freezing rain and come straight back in again. Fortunately, it didn't happen every night and, I thought, still much better than the effort required to put her in her kennel for the night.

A long two weeks later, the bandages came off and Olly was nearly as good as new, minus half a back toe. Life could get back to "normal" in the rotty house.

A week into the stay I had a phone call from our owners. "We think Megan," one of the spaniels, "might come into season whilst you are there. Please watch her if she does and don't let her out of your sight."

"Great, I thought!" Just what I needed.

All five of "our" dogs were female but we were surrounded by farms with hordes of randy male dogs of all descriptions. We'd had a similar problem with Sooty, another of the spaniels, on a previous visit. Both Sooty and Megan were two expensive and very efficient gun dogs and were used for breeding more of the same. Our owners certainly would not be pleased to find Megan producing labraspaniels some time after we had gone.

I knew vaguely what to look for in Megan and I saw no tell tale signs, but then I'm no expert. I was not too concerned, however, and anyway the dogs did not usually stray off the property even if the gate was left open. The spaniels all had their own whistles to which they obediently responded. One, two or three blasts, depending on what you wanted them to do. All were at different pitches and once I'd mastered whose was which it was easy.

However, and there always seems to be one, just when things seem to be going smoothly, Megan disappeared one morning for about two hours. I called and whistled in the garden, in the surrounding fields and round the lakes. Nothing. Muttering a few choice words under my breath, I rounded up the other dogs, put them in their kennels, locked up the house and jumped in the Range Rover to start searching.

I called at about five or six "nearby" houses but no one had seen Megan. I whistled and called her name all over the surrounding area but to no avail. I left my phone number with people, although being a rural community, most of them knew the dog and its owners anyway.

I returned home dog-less and sure enough, not long after, Megan appeared, covered in mud, out of breath and looking as though she'd had a great time. Not too great, I hoped.

Now I was really worried. I didn't think Megan was in season but I couldn't be sure. I pondered for a while and thought, "What would the owners do, or what would I do if I was Megan's owner?"

I'd get the dog checked out. So, I took another executive decision on behalf of Megan's owners and phoned the vet. Funnily enough a different practice to the one to which I had taken Olly. Rumour had it that they were scared of Rottweilers! No, I didn't believe it either.

The vet was very understanding regarding my position, and Megan's, and suggested that it would be a good idea first to check whether she was in season before doing anything drastic like administering "the day after birth control for dogs".

As it happens, I learned, the morning after treatment is actually three days after for dogs so I made an appointment for Megan on the coming Saturday, this being Thursday. Saturday arrived and Megan ended up on the vet's table after having first peed on the waiting room floor to my embarrassment. Another patient's owner had made a great fuss of her and I guess it was mixture of excitement and fear that caused Megan to lose control. I took her outside immediately she had done it and was surprised that the other owner had cleaned it up when we returned. She must have felt guilty.

The vet did a visual and took some swabs and we went home to wait the results. He called later that day and gave us the all clear, Megan did not appear to be in season. Thankfully, on their return, her owners agreed that I had taken the right course of action.

We'd been looking after Olly and the various spaniels for over eight years. We knew her well and had been with her in some of her finest and worst moments. We'd seen her in her energetic youth, clearing double stiles in one bound and almost able to keep up with the spaniels as they ran free in the open fields. Her pure strength; the glistening black coat and rippling muscles, aggressive when she needed to be but gentle and loving with those she knew and trusted.

We'd nursed her through illness and injury. I'll never forget the biscuit, muzzle and boot routine and we always felt safe and secure in the knowledge that Olly was out there patrolling the grounds at night. There were times, as she was getting much older, and when the temperature was forecast to be well below zero at night we relaxed the rules and let her sleep beside the Aga. We never told her owners but, when they read this, we don't think they'll mind.

The day came when we drove away from the house down the long lane to the outside world, after staying with Olly for another five weeks, that we knew we would not see her again. Olly had had a growth in her mouth for some time and was in pretty obvious discomfort and pain. The vet had said there was nothing they could do and that it was just a matter of time.

Sue and I both had tears in our eyes and it was difficult to leave her. She had given us so much pleasure and companionship over the years and we were so sad to hear a week or so later that Olly had taken that final trip to the vet.

It was as though another chapter in our life had ended.

Chapter Five

The Faith Healer

Of all the good things about the house sitting "business", the chance to stay in a wide variety of other peoples' houses and to share their magnificent gardens, outlooks and views was the most interesting. As we love the countryside and its history, it gave us a real chance to explore other parts of the country. One particular house in the Yorkshire Dales was among the best in this respect. One balmy July evening we sat on the patio looking south over the river Ure, which meandered gracefully through the valley below towards the old market town of Middleham and its historic castle. We marvelled at the fact that it was not costing us a penny to be there. Similar accommodation would have cost the earth if we had rented it on holiday.

This particular time we were on another five-week "assignment" while the owners were away on a trip to Australia. Our charges were an ageing Labrador called Ben, a young Labrador named Josie, a sort of wire haired Jack Russell and two cats. Oh, I must not forget the fish. A small stream ran down one side of the garden and had been cleverly diverted through a pond in which lived some sizeable gold fish. The garden was enclosed on three sides by a traditional dry-stone wall, built by the son of the owner.

From the garden we could see the gallops on the tops of hills far across the Ure valley where, often just after dawn, we would see strings of horses from the famous stables of Middleham exercising in the early morning mists. It is said that the monks of nearby Jervaulx Abbey probably started the horse breeding and training in the fourteenth century that made Middleham a horse racing centre long before Newmarket in Suffolk. The Abbey dates back to the 12th century and had stood for nearly three hundred years before its destruction. Well worth a visit but not much of the structure remains today, due to the greed of Henry VIII.

However, a good part of Middleham castle is still standing and it is rich in history. There is evidence that there had been a fortified structure on or near the site since the days of Alan the Red in 1069. The Neville family acquired the castle through marriage in the 13th century and made it the "Windsor of the North". King Richard the Third then took it over in 1471 and his son, Edward, was born and died there.

Regrettably, although some of the castle was dismantled in 1646, the keep, which dates back to the 1170s, still stands almost to its full height. We climbed to the top of the keep during a late afternoon visit and imagined what might have happened in the castle during its time as a royal residence so far removed from London. The walls of the great halls and banqueting chamber survive today. In the early evening sunshine that day it was not difficult to imagine the royal party and their guests, often more than 200 in number, gathered in their finery at the huge tables that would have stood in the now empty shell. Long ago it must have been such an impressive sight in that splendid building.

Each day during our stay we took the dogs for walks along the banks of the river. Whilst Ben would walk slowly and with some difficulty behind us, Josie, full of the excitement and energy of youth, would chase rabbits and hurtle in and out of the river after ducks and other water birds. Sand Martins dive-bombed us as we disturbed their natural habitat and water rats scurried back into their holes as we passed.

It was always difficult to exercise young and old dogs together. So, on occasion, as we did at other locations with dogs of vastly differing ages, we would leave old Ben behind in order to let Josie have a real run and a much longer walk.

Josie was expected to come into season while we were in residence so we had instructions to take her to, and I quote, "be married" should this happen. We looked for the telltale signs each day but fortunately we were spared the embarrassment, and the long trip some 40 miles away, of having to take Josie to see her "husband".

Ben the Labrador had advanced cancer and was in quite a bad way. He was on medication and had had several bad turns. His condition was so serious that his owners did not expect him to survive during their absence. In addition to the usual telephone numbers left for us, i.e. vet, plumber etc, we also had the number to ring if Ben died so that he could be buried in the right spot on their property.

Old Ben and friends!

A bit daunting really, but we'd seen nearly everything before (or so we thought) so we took it all in our stride and waved the family goodbye. We could tell by the tears, particularly from the children, that they really did not expect to see Ben again.

Along with the medication, some of it homeopathic and the strict diet and exercise instructions, we had been amazed to receive a request to take Ben (a Labrador, remember) to a faith healer twice during our stay. Remembering Jason, my twelve and a half year old Labrador who eventually had to take the one-way trip to the vet some years ago, I could sympathise with the "try anything" attitude of Ben's owners. Still, it did seem rather strange, particularly as Ben's owner was a vet, and we looked forward to the appointed day with great interest.

In the meantime we followed Ben's owners' instructions to the letter, took him for limited exercise and showered him with all the care and attention due to a respected senior citizen. We were glad to see that his condition did not deteriorate and, indeed, some days after our arrival his coat improved, he was walking with less discomfort and he was generally more cheerful. He was always pleased to see us and, increasingly, he enjoyed his food.

As his owners had told us that he had had a bad spell after his last visit to the faith healer (I shall call her Madame X) we were more than apprehensive that his next visit might do the same.

The day came. We helped Ben into the car and set off further up into the Dales for his treatment. We drove northwards down winding lanes through the beautiful Yorkshire countryside in the height of summer. Away to the right we could see the coast with the sun sparkling off the sea and the commercial buildings and chimneys of Teesside. Only the distance involved softened the harsh views of the nuclear power station and other heavy industrial plants of this stretch of coastline.

To our left, the Dales rose away eastward into the distance. This was real James Herriot country. Dry-stone walls marched across the rolling fields as far as the eye could see, punctuated only by the occasional stone-built barn and solid looking farmhouse built to withstand the strong cold winds of winter that often raked across this, often bleak, landscape. It all looked as though this had been the scene here for hundreds of years with little change. It probably had.

Hardy, hefted sheep dotted the sloping windswept fields providing a good measure of contrast with the green of the grass, the grey stonework and the deep blue sky. There are not many places on earth that match the quiet beauty of the Yorkshire Dales and I include the countryside of Africa, New Zealand, North America and even Scotland in my comparison.

Not that I am from these parts. Far from it. I was born a man of Kent or a Kentish man - I can never remember which. Maidstone was nearer my place of birth than Gillingham, if that means anything to those well versed in Kentish folklore. Perhaps someone will let me know.

I digress. We found our destination with little trouble and learned that Madame X provided her services in an upstairs flat in a large and beautiful old country house surrounded by mature gardens. Next door was a village cricket pitch and a quiet patch of woodland.

We had to park outside the garden gates, as there was only a green footpath leading up to the house, no drive.

Madame X ushered us into her consulting room as if Ben's visit was quite a normal procedure and as though she had been treating dogs all her life. There were the obligatory reference books, colourful curtains, oriental rugs on the floor, crystals in the window and Madame X herself was dressed in flowing robes and earrings. In the corner was a couch obviously for the use of her clients.

Trying to be helpful, as ever, I offered to lift Ben on to the couch for his "consultation". She glanced at me, gave me a withering, scornful look, reserved no doubt for the unbelievers, and said that, "Ben would be all right on the floor, thank you very much".

Sue did not help the situation by asking, "Do you do people too?"

"I **do** people," she said, haughtily.

Suitably chastened, Sue and I sat down. This was a whole new experience for us.

"You are quite welcome to stay in the room", Madame X said, "but please do not interrupt, whatever happens. Ben must have absolute peace and quiet and be as relaxed as possible."

"OK," we mumbled and sat as still and as quiet as we could, on some very uncomfortable wooden, three legged stools, I might add, while Madame X started her "treatment". It began with several minutes of meditation whilst Ben simply lay quite still on the floor, breathed heavily and slipped off into a deep sleep. Well, when you are the human equivalent of about ninety-ten years old, you've had your pills and a good breakfast, a walk, an hour's drive in the car on a warm summer's day and you've been invited to take a lie down you would, wouldn't you?

The meditation over, Madame X gently laid her hands on Ben's head for a few minutes and then on his swollen stomach where the cancer was quite evident. The old dog did not stir.

Next, she held her hands palms down about an inch or two above Ben's head and moved them slowly, without making contact with his coat, down the full length of his body. Then carefully and with a definitely artistic, demonstrative flourish she slowly wrung her hands in the air behind Ben's rear end.

Being relatively astute people, we realised immediately that this was getting rid of the evil demons in Ben's body and that it must be well worth the money and the travelling to have this carried out every two weeks.

This exercise was repeated several times and she crossed her hands occasionally with different degrees of artistic hand movement and "rinsing". You could almost feel the pressure building and I was sure something magical was about to occur.

Sure enough, it did. Ben gave a big sigh and let out a huge, satisfied fart.

Sue looked at me as if to say (remember, we were sworn to silence) "Was that you?"

I shook my head violently and we both had great difficulty in suppressing guffaws of laughter. Madame X appeared not to have heard and carried on as though either nothing had happened, or that this was a perfectly normal occurrence. We had the feeling that, indeed, it must have happened before.

Still dead to the world and, seemingly with a smile on his face, Ben passed wind again but our unmovable practitioner carried on oblivious to the sounds, and the odour!

At last, the session came to an end and we took our leave. Madame X asked us if we were going to pay for Ben's sessions but we responded that we had not been asked to do so by his owners. Madame X would therefore have to submit her bill to them on their return. During this exchange we found out how much she charged for her services and we realised immediately that if we ever became really hard up we had found a new career that we were now fully qualified upon which to embark!

Ben didn't seem any worse, or better, for his experience and as we walked through the garden to the car I said, perhaps a little too loudly, "What a load of mumbo jumbo."

Not that I have anything against faith healers for people you understand. I just think that for dogs.... Well, surely you can understand what I mean!

On the way home we stopped by a stream for Ben to do what old male dogs often have to do and we were delighted to see that he was strong enough to go into the water and actually swim around for a while. Maybe there was something in faith healing for dogs after all.

On our next visit to Madame X two weeks later I was politely asked whether I would care to remain in the garden during the treatment! She even offered me a spade to do some digging, "If I felt like it."

Politely, I declined the offer and spent a very pleasant half hour sitting in the sunshine soaking up the atmosphere in that beautiful country house garden. Breathing the pure north Yorkshire air, listening to the birds and the insects humming I thought, as I often did, how much more pleasant this was compared to risking my life in the rush-hour traffic of Riyadh each day. Similarly, it certainly beat driving on the M25, that concrete car park that passes for the motorway surrounding London.

Sue was permitted to sit in at the second session, however, and later assured me that much the same thing had occurred as on our previous visit.

By the end of the five weeks Ben had improved markedly and was jumping up and running around almost like a puppy. He was walking longer distances and with greater ease. On their return, his owners were amazed and delighted at his improvement. Whether it was the faith healer, our care and attention during that five weeks or a combination of both, we'll never know.

This all happened in the July of that year. Sadly, we had a call from Ben's owners in September advising that he had died peacefully. On many occasions afterwards we stopped by Ben's grave whilst walking the other dogs on subsequent visits and remembered with affection our brief acquaintance with a fine old dog – and the strange faith healer affair.

On a happier note, Josie and her "husband" had later met successfully and one of their offspring, Berti, was now in residence as a hyperactive, but intellectually challenged, yellow male puppy. His main claim to fame was sitting on top of his long-suffering mother at every opportunity.

Perhaps he inherited this trait from her, as her party piece was to lock herself in the broom/boot cupboard where she loved to lie on top of assorted wellies, walking boots and trainers. If she was ever lost that was the first place we would look. Maybe she liked the smell!

We never went back to that house after first meeting Bertie so we don't know how he progressed in life but we did miss old Ben and the other dogs and that wonderful Yorkshire Dales setting.

Chapter Six

The Sheep

You might remember that Pagan, a golden retriever, and his friend, Gunner, featured briefly early on in this saga. Pagan was the one who followed us home on the golf course during our first house sit. Two years after that unexpected encounter we received a call from his owner asking us if we could come down to East Sussex from Yorkshire and look after their dogs for two weeks in February.

Horrors! We were already booked for part of that time but only about seven miles away from Pagan's house. If we could bear a one- week overlap we could do both, so we agreed to take on the job. Pagan was such a good natured handsome dog that we really could not refuse.

On the appointed day we arrived for our "briefing" and after learning of the dogs' and cats' requirements, the lady of the house said, "What do you know about sheep?"

We had known that she had a number of Jacobs' show sheep in the grounds but we did not know that some of them were in lamb and would possibly deliver during our stay. We recalled our time in Devon and, reassured by the presence of various charts, instructions, vet's phone numbers and the presence of an experienced "lamber" living quite close by, we assured her that everything would be all right. We had helped with lambing in Devon many times.

So, we now had two dogs, two cats and twelve sheep to care for in the middle of winter and I was to be seven miles away for a week looking after two boisterous flat coat retriever puppies, their mother and a cat. We organised the logistics of shopping, where we would be eating meals, who would be staying in which house and where we would meet up to walk various sets of dogs.

We were again in my sister's neck of the woods, Ashdown Forest, and there were her two dogs (and various boarders), together with her neighbours and their dogs to bear in mind on communal walks. It was never easy, as some dogs did not get on with others and had to be kept apart. The flat coat retriever puppies were not to go for walks or meet other dogs until they were older and, of course, we always made it a rule not to be away from any house or dogs for longer than absolutely necessary.

I think the largest number of dogs we ever had on a single walk across the Forest was fifteen! Although there were four people in "control" it was difficult to keep track of who was where and who wasn't. There were always stragglers and roamers and those that ran on ahead in addition to the socialisers who would run off with other groups of dogs and to investigate other people's picnics! We never lost any dogs though, on any of our walks!

This episode in our career was in a year when severe thunderstorms raged across the south east of England that February. When don't they?

One night at around four in the morning the house I was in was struck by lightning. The flat coat retrievers were going berserk, the lightning had taken out the electricity supply and I was worried that the chimney had come off, or worse. Having calmed down the dogs as best I could, by torch light I set about finding the mains electricity supply to restore power.

One of the cardinal rules of house sitting was to establish where essentials like fuse boxes, water stop cocks and central heating controls are located before you actually need them. I knew where the fuse box was but I had to move a hall coat stand and mirror to get to it!

Doesn't sound too bad, does it? But when you've three dogs barking, you're in the dark in someone else's house at four o'clock in the morning and there's the mother of all thunderstorms raging overhead, it's slightly off-putting. It didn't help matters when on resetting the circuit breaker the intruder alarm burst into action from all angles. Lights flashing, alarm sounding, three big dogs barking, pandemonium! A quick trawl of the memory, number recalled, where's the control panel? Number keyed in, and peace restored. I doubt whether any of the neighbours noticed a thing as the storm was still crashing around above.

Meanwhile, as they say, seven miles away back at the house where Sue was staying, she also had been awakened by the storm. Fearful for the enceinte ewes, she was out in her wellies checking the sheep, which she had done every night, but not at that hour, or in a howling windswept raging thunderstorm. Remember it was February, not August or September, so the rain was not far off freezing point. On this occasion peering through the pouring rain into a paddock starkly lit by continuous lightning, Sue counted heads, with great difficulty and realised that there were more sheep than there should have been.

Twins had arrived earlier during the night without a problem but they were now in danger of drowning where they lay. The immediate task was to take them into the nearby barn, clean them up and pen them away from the rest of the sheep. So there was Sue, on her own, in night clothes, by torch light, in the middle of the storm picking up soaking lambs, making sure she'd selected the right ewe, rubbing the lambs against their mother and slowly carrying the lambs into the barn hoping mother would follow.

The four of them, Sue, the mother and the two lambs, struggled quietly and carefully through the mud and the crashing storm, up the hilly, tussock-strewn paddock and towards the open fronted barn. Inside, there were pens readied with straw bales, water buckets and hay nets. Sue carefully carried the two lambs whilst she opened a metal gate and, continually nudged by an anxious mother, she managed to put all three into the comparative comfort and warmth of the previously prepared barn.

It wasn't easy but it worked. After settling them in, it was necessary to wipe their umbilical cords with disinfectant and check that the cords had been chewed off. Normally the mother would do this naturally, in addition to undertaking all the cleaning of the lambs, and herself. This, even in the hostile environments in which many sheep have their lambs, particularly out on the fells up against the long dry-stone walls of the Yorkshire moors or the hedges of lowland farms.

After the necessary ablutions and minor medical treatments had been administered, Sue retired again to bed, cold and wet but thrilled to have been part of the process. The lambs were left for the rest of the night to bond with their mother. The next day necessitated the ear tagging. As these were top quality show sheep, Sue was anxious that all should be well when their owners returned. Happily, mother and children were doing fine on the return of their owners from their camel trek across the Sinai desert.

Fortunately, no more midwifery was required during the rest of Sue's stay but she did have a repeat performance another year. The second time she was more prepared for the vicissitudes of weather and sheep. The procedure went without a hitch again until she realised that one of a pair of twins was not suckling the morning after its birth. Firstly, Sue tried putting the little lamb right up against the ewe's teat thinking that it, as yet, had not realised what it was supposed to do! That didn't work. The lamb still showed no inclination to suck. Next, she held the mother's teat up against the lamb's mouth, but still it showed no interest. Now, one can hand rear lambs but it is a very time consuming process and they fare so much better on their mothers' milk. So, another try was made.

Sue found a lamb feeding bottle, a rubber teat and stainless steel bowl and then, bowl in hand, went into the sheep pen and knelt by the ewe. With the bowl strategically placed she started feeling for the distended teat! Now, if you have never milked a cow, never mind a sheep, and all you have to go on is the James Herriot stories and The Great Yorkshire Show milking demonstrations, this task was to be a revelation. However, it was not as difficult as they would have you believe or, maybe, to some it comes naturally!

Within just a few minutes Sue had enough to partially fill the bottle and soon the lamb was sucking greedily. Then with a little guile and delicate manoeuvring, Sue brought the lamb's nose up to the mother's teat again and voila, it was soon suckling from its mother. After that, the lamb had no problems and went from strength to strength.

Meanwhile, back at "my" place, my spell with the flat coats was coming to an end. Just as well, as I had had little sleep. Their room was directly below mine and they seemed to delight in keeping me awake most of the night. Despite that, they were beautiful and full of fun. One of the puppies went to a new owner but we still looked after mother and one daughter from time to time. I'm happy to say that both mother and daughter had quieted down considerably and were a great pleasure to be around.

Pagan and Gunner were also a great delight to look after. As Pagan was prone to wander, we took especial care when out walking with him and he never strayed for long while in our charge.

However, some time later we were in the locality again staying in two other houses. Sue had the car and she came to pick me up to go out for a pub lunch – it was our wedding anniversary - when she saw Pagan trotting along a main road about three miles from his house. Sue had just passed Pagan's owner's car parked on the Forest so she assumed that he had gone walkabout and was on his way home. As it was an extremely busy road Sue stopped, called to Pagan, opened the back hatch of the car and he quite readily jumped in. He was not wearing his collar. Sue turned the car around, returned to the owner's car in one of the car parks on Ashdown Forest and waited for a while before writing a note, which she left on the windscreen and then left to pick me up.

When she arrived Sue explained to me why Pagan was in the car. I patted him and said, "Hi Pagan," as you do, to him and off we set for his house on our way to the pub. As we drove up the winding drive through their delightful gardens towards the house we saw, with some relief, that Pagan's owner's car was in the garage but, horrors, we were shocked to see Pagan in the back of the car!

It was immediately obvious that Sue had picked up a Pagan look-alike! We let our unidentified dog out of the car. Pagan jumped out of his and once they were side by side we could see straight away that "our" dog was a year or two younger and a little smaller than Pagan. In fact, on closer inspection, we saw that it was a bitch! An excusable lapse in gender recognition, I hasten to add, due to both dogs having extremely long, shaggy coats! We felt a little embarrassed explaining the situation to Pagan's owners but, as doggy people, they understood and we telephoned the police and then the local dog warden.

As we were by now running late for our pre-booked lunch we left the dog at Pagan's house and on checking later we were relieved to find that not only had the warden collected the dog, the owner had contacted the warden and the dog was back at home. Sue had been worried that she might have picked up the dog from outside its own front gate but it had been lost on the Forest and the owner lived some distance away. Hopefully, it had slipped its collar and was not being walked without one. Foolish, to say the least, if it had not been wearing a collar, no matter how well trained the dog might be.

****

It was great to keep in touch with so many dogs. In so many ways it was much better than having dogs of our own. Although we didn't have the constant fun and companionship that dogs can bring, we had access to a far greater variety and we felt as though we knew and loved them all even, or perhaps especially, Olly the rotty.

The greatest benefit to us was that we had the freedom to travel for months at a time if we wanted without having to get someone to look after dogs of our own or, heaven forbid, put them into kennels. Not that I have anything against the kennel or cattery industry. Far from it. They provide an important facility for owners to board their pets whilst away and an essential service for those animals coming to the UK from overseas. It is almost certain that our quarantine laws, no matter how strict we might think they were, have kept Britain free of rabies over the years. The vast majority of kennels are clean, well run and their staffs look after their charges with great care. We even know of one establishment that provides radio and television for their "guests". The "rooms" even have wallpaper.

I can just hear you saying, "That has to be in a wacky part of California."

You would be wrong; but not too far off the mark. It is located in a rather smart part of Naples, Florida, and is very popular with the locals. However, no matter how well equipped the kennel, how attentive and loving the staff and which TV channels they are allowed to watch, we still believe that pets are happier left in their own, familiar environment whilst their owners are away.

Chapter Seven

The Spice Of Life

We found over the years that we became "experts" in various fields through our experiences in different homes and gardens. Variety had been the key word since the day we started. In all, during our dog sitting, we stayed in around two dozen houses of different shapes and sizes ranging from the quite small, but in beautiful locations, to huge places with more bathrooms than the average large house has bedrooms. From this, and our own former somewhat nomadic lifestyle we gained a pretty good idea of what we wanted in terms of house size and design. In addition to our "dog houses", Sue and I had had homes in eleven different places since we teamed up together. Over the years we took the best ideas from all of our houses, coupled them with those of our own and came up with our perfect des res which, as yet, is still on paper but will hopefully one day be transmitted into bricks and mortar, timber frame or even stone.

We've both always been keen on gardening and our way of life certainly allowed us to enjoy some beautiful gardens along the way. Some might think it strange, however, that we paid a gardener handsomely to look after our own garden at home but we often kept other people's tidy, for free! What could be better though, to know that you didn't really have to work in the garden but could if you wanted to?

I hesitate to stray too much into gardening hints or advice here but it is amazing how some people did let things get out of hand in their gardens. Weeds are always best dealt with before they become a major problem. In the same vein as "a stitch in time saves nine", one of my favourite gardening adages is, "the more you hoe, the less you have to." I'll say no more!

We met more than one person along the way who kept their regular gardeners on only out of a sense of loyalty or compassion and one who even hid specific tools from the gardener to prevent unnecessary pruning and trimming!

Some folks were on very good terms with their gardeners, even allowing them into the house to make their own tea or coffee in their absence. One couple regularly had their gardener/handy man in to lunch at the kitchen table with them and shared a bottle of wine with him. I should say that they are the nicest pair of folk we have met in our travels and it was always a pleasure to visit them when we were in the area, even if we were not looking after their house. I won't embarrass them by mentioning their names here but they'll know who they are!

Others we know never even supplied refreshments, wishing to maintain class differentials I suppose. Often we supplied the tea, coffee and biscuits out of our own provisions, especially on long stays, but we didn't mind that one bit.

Our conversations provided us with a wealth of local colour and knowledge that we could not have gleaned elsewhere. Quite often we would hear tidbits of gossip from staff that they should not really have told us but we always maintained absolute discretion and never passed on any potentially embarrassing information about our clients, many of whom knew each other and shared the same domestic staff. It's funny how people did gossip though, especially when their livelihoods might be on the line if their indiscretions had got back to their employers.

Talking of hospitality, we found most of our owners very generous in terms of leaving us wine and food for our stays. Some said, "Just help yourselves."

That was a little risky, considering our liking for good food and wine. Most, however, left us varying amounts of wine ranging from the remnants of open bottles to half a dozen, or more. We did have some strange ones, like a twenty-odd year old bottle of Californian Chardonnay. Maybe 1980 was a good year, but we did not fancy the thought. We e-mailed the vineyard on that one, asking whether it would still be in good enough condition to drink after all these years. To our surprise, they even replied.

"Sure," they said, "it might still be OK but have another bottle on standby just in case it isn't."

It was not, and we did.

This next tale does not necessarily apply to our house owners, but have you ever thought that the most generous people are usually those less well off? For many years, I was a member of Lions International, a large charity organization, which exists in cities, towns and villages all over the world. One of the many things we used to do was call house-to-house just before Christmas to collect packeted and canned food to parcel up for needy people in the local community.

We would drop leaflets through letterboxes a few days in advance and then knock on doors to collect the goods. Over the years, I found that you could almost predict the outcome depending on the affluence of the neighbourhood. The "haul" would be very thin in the more up market areas and, with a few exceptions, the poorer areas would be more generous. One striking experience reflected this.

We called at one small bungalow in a less affluent area of the town one night. A little old woman came to the door, obviously a hard up pensioner, and greeted us warmly. She had read our earlier note, and was so enthusiastic about what we were doing that she felt she had to contribute. She chatted to us for a while and then tried to press a whole basket of food upon us. From her clothes and the general appearance of her house, it was obvious that she did not really have two pennies to rub together. It was very difficult tactfully to refuse some of her offerings without offending her. We think we managed it and came away feeling quite humbled that someone in her position would want to give so generously to those she thought were less well off than her.

I digress again, but I hope, with a tale that might make you think how lucky most of us are and that there are still some really good people left in the world.

Regarding hospitality, we did draw the line, however, at one location where we had been asked to prepare meals for a locum vet staying in the same house. It wasn't the food that caused the problem, as we were recompensed for that and Sue loves cooking and entertaining anyway. But I took a dim view of the vet's appetite for my gin and tonic before dinner and glasses of our wine during our meals.

Without warning on one occasion at the same house we were expected to take after hours telephone calls for the vet as the locum had not been engaged. We were not very pleased about that and together with the piles of dirty socks and trainers on the bedroom window-sills that was the last straw.

The same people, on more than one occasion, left us with the debris from large dinner parties to wash up. Needless of me to tell you, we soon came to the decision that we should politely decline future invitations to return to that house.

At another place, we were left in no doubt about the value and fragility of several hundred pieces of Staffordshire Pottery about the house. The owners were away for four weeks but we could only look after their home and dogs for the first three. The arrangement was to be that their daughter and son-in-law would handle the fourth week. We learned that they would be bringing their large Labrador and a small child with them, which gave us cause for alarm about the porcelain.

We hit on the ideal solution. I took digital photographs of all the pieces in their original positions and set the camera to record the time and date. We therefore had proof that on the day we left the premises all was well with their precious pottery.

This was also the household that counted the cutlery after we left. Not the silver cutlery, but the common-or-garden, not even stainless steel, stuff for everyday use in the kitchen. We quite often took carving or bread knives with us on our house sits, along with other favourite utensils with which Sue prefers to cook. In addition, on that occasion as on many others, Sue had taken a whole raft of kitchen equipment and cutlery with her to use during an away from home Aga demonstration. We had inadvertently walked away with one of the ordinary kitchen knives but were slightly surprised that the kitchen cutlery had been counted after we left. Maybe we should have signed an inventory! However, we didn't pinch the wooden spoon, which allegedly, was also missing.

I suspected the Labrador.

We did bring the knife back all the way from Yorkshire to East Sussex on our next trip south! We didn't go back there again either.

Our away from home gardening was enjoyable, educational and a wonderful source of some unusual cuttings here and there to take home to fill the odd spot in our own garden.

During my time, I have probably used more ride-on mowers than most, barring the professional gardener, and along with dog walking, we enjoyed our outdoor labours as one way to help us keep fit. Along the way, I found that essential equipment for a good lawn included a good, well-maintained, mower and a sharp set of long-handled clippers. Given the choice, for large lawns I would go for a front mounted blade assembly on a rear steering ride-on mower allowing a cut unaffected by the wheel tracks and better manoeuvrability. On a smaller lawn a cylinder blade with a rear roller provided the best finish. Rotary mowers and Flymos were great where there might be accessibility problems, rough ground, longer grass or slopes, but the finish was never as good.

However, it was not just outdoor pursuits and interests through which we increased our knowledge of machinery, tools or appliances. We had our moments with more mundane, everyday indoor items as well.

We had thought that ours was the only temperamental toaster in the world. Not so! You would be amazed at the variety of toasters out there with minds of their own. There are those that ejected toast on to the worktop or floor as soon as you turned your back, those that went straight from white to burnt, those that refused to give up the toast at any stage and those that achieved a combination of all of the above. By far the best method and most reliable we found was the good old Aga cooker and the toasting bat. Even I managed successfully to toast bread on an Aga!

A polite word of warning here, though. As it is probably the quickest toasting method known to man, short of using a real fire, a constant watch needs to be kept to avoid cinder toast! On a really hot Aga it's best to leave the lid up so you can see the first hint of smoke! I became quite adept at toasting on the "hot" hot plate and poaching eggs on the other one whilst boiling a kettle at the same time. Don't forget to pre-heat the toasting bat either if you want to avoid the bread sticking to it, and cut the bread quite thickly to avoid it slipping out of the bat whilst turning it over!

Most of "our" houses had either Agas or Rayburns much to Sue's delight as she put her training and skills as an Aga freelance demonstrator to good use in producing many excellent meals along the way. I don't know of any better form of heating/cooking than the Aga or Rayburn for providing a central source of warmth and that homely country feeling especially in older, larger houses.

A cast iron wood burner also would be one of my favourite sources of heat in, for example dining rooms or family rooms. However, there can be nothing better that a traditional open log fire particularly when set in a large stone "walk-in" fireplace complete with inglenooks and a bread oven. Very romantic on a cold winter's night. We did come across one wood burner which had the best of both worlds. Having large double-hinged doors at the front, almost the whole width of the fire, it was to all intents and purposes an open fire with the doors fully open. The Dovre 2300 will be the one for us.

In one old house in Sussex the wood burning stove in the dining room caused us a more than a little consternation on one visit. The owners had left on a Thursday and, due to other commitments, we could not get there until the following Sunday. The home help had therefore been recruited to look in on the house every day and my sister had volunteered to look after the dog at her house until we arrived. We always looked after this house in July so we had never used this particular stove and, in fact, neither had the owners as they had just replaced their old one with a brand new specimen.

We had only been in the house a few minutes and were still unloading the car when I heard a strange faint scratching sound coming from the fireplace in the dining room. It only lasted a few seconds, and then it stopped. I was puzzled but didn't think too much about it and carried on bringing our things into the house. It wasn't long before I heard it again.

"Did you hear that?" I said to Sue.

Of course she hadn't and she thought that I was imagining things. Old houses sometimes do produce inexplicable noises but usually at night. This was mid-afternoon.

It happened again and this time we both heard it. The wood burner was alive! Or, at least that's where the sound appeared to be coming from. It didn't take us long to deduce that there was something trapped inside and that it was probably a bird. Easy, I thought. We'd dealt with incidents of this sort before.

We opened windows, closed doors, took all ornaments off tables, window-sills and shelves and moved anything else we thought might get damaged when we opened the stove doors and set the bird free. I quietly opened the door expecting a flurry of wings but nothing at all happened. Not a bird in sight.

We found a torch and peered into the stove. Not a sign of a bird or anything other than a neatly laid fire waiting for the first cool nights of autumn. Still, we could hear a faint scratching and at last we realized that it was coming from the flue immediately above the stove. On looking up through the doorway and into the chimney we could see the vague outline of feathers above a grille between the flue and the fire chamber.

Now the question was how to get the bird out before it died and started to cause offence to senses other than our hearing! There were four bolts securing the grille to the casing of the firebox but it looked like a tricky job without having to dismantle other parts of the stove. I really did not want to have to dismantle their new stove even though it was relatively clean, never having been used, and I could have probably found all the tools I needed. Just as I was resigning myself to having to take the thing to pieces we noticed a metal band round the flue pipe, I noticed that it had been cleverly fitted so as to appear almost invisible from the front. It had a clip at the rear holding it tightly in place around the chimney.

I unclipped the band and lowered it to reveal a six inch hole at the front of the flue. For a while nothing happened. Then, very slowly, a soot-covered head appeared which we identified as belonging to a jackdaw. Its eyes blinked at the light, it staggered out of the chimney, landed awkwardly on top of the stove and promptly fell on to the floor. Our precautions to prevent damage by a frightened bird skittering around the room were unnecessary. This bird was too weak to fly.

Later, we quizzed the home help about it and she said that she had heard something on the Friday during her visit that day. So the poor creature had been trapped in the dark without food or water for at least two full days!

I picked up the bird and took it outside and placed it gently in the shade of one of the shrubberies. Before I could go and get it water it shambled off and disappeared from view. We never saw it again and presumed, hopefully, that it survived its ordeal.

****

Many of our houses boasted long case clocks, or other valuable antique timepieces and our responsibilities often included keeping these running during our stay. We can therefore now claim to be second only to the Antiques Road Show staff in our knowledge of these wonderful objects. We never knew there were so many different types of movements and winding methods. In the immortal words of the Remington shaver company owner, we liked them so much we eventually bought one; a magnificent long case, which now stands regally in our own hall. We have also acquired a beautiful Viennese regulator, which adorns one of our sitting room walls.

However, when we were residing in some of our "country homes", clocks with loud chimes were sometimes more than a minor nuisance. Especially when situated at the bottom of the stairs or in rooms below our bedroom.

We therefore became well versed in methods of suppressing the chimes. Of course, by far the simplest methods were merely to switch off the chiming mechanism, to stop the pendulum or not to wind them up! However immobilizing the clock was not practicable on clocks that displayed the date, phases of the moon and other such extremely useful information. In addition, if we didn't stop the clock in the right place, i.e. just before the time we needed to start it again, we had to spend a good deal of time and care moving the hands past each chiming point until we reached the correct time. That could be a lengthy job with clocks that chimed four times an hour!

One particularly loud long case clock defied all attempts to turn off its chimes. As a last resort, but with great care, we had to employ the strategic placement of two layers of sticking plaster on the bell routine. The chimes sounded as a dull thud, not the hitherto shrill ding and we slept peacefully for the rest of our stay.

Around noon one day during that visit we had an unexpected visitor, a friend of the owners. We were talking in the hall as the top of the noon hour approached. We dreaded her hearing the muted chimes - it was a valuable clock, after all. We steered her into the study, talked a little more enthusiastically, the hour struck, the strangled chimes went unnoticed and we breathed again. Needless to say, we did remember to remove the surgical appliance in good time before our owners returned.

We were in a downstairs bedroom at another house one time, right next to the dining room with a chiming clock just the other side of the wall. It was as though Big Ben was about a foot away from our heads. We cured that problem by laying the clock down whereupon it went "to sleep". The time mechanism still functioned but the chimes went into hold mode until the clock was righted each morning. Strangely enough the number of chimes still coincided with the correct time.

One medium sized clock I "put to sleep" did cause me a particular problem. When I came to stand it up again the pendulum fell to pieces. Now, all my life I've been pretty good at taking things apart and putting them back together again. Despite what Sue says! After all, for the first ten years of my working career I used to work on jet aircraft engines and never had one fall out of the sky as a result of my efforts!

However, this pendulum I had not taken apart in the first place and there were at least four intricate pieces which had no visible means of support, fixing and no logical structure. Trial and error has always been one of the key roads to success and it only took me an hour or so to get it back together again. The clock worked. Kept good time too, after that, much to my surprise and great relief!

For smaller clocks where chimes could not be silenced, the bury-it-under-the-cushions method always worked and a good night's sleep was the reward. I was often tempted to try the same on various church tower clocks!

(Author's note: No clocks were actually harmed during the compiling of this book!)

Well, that's not quite true actually. I did once have the misfortune to over-wind one particularly fine clock. Whilst raising one of the weights my attention was distracted and I failed to notice that the pulley wheel was fast approaching its attachment point. Before I could do anything there was a twang, the cord broke and the weight came crashing down on to the bottom of the casing. As it descended it hit the other weight and damaged its ornate brass top.

I felt sick. There was no way I could repair the damage, the cord was of a special type, it was broken such that it could not be knotted and access to the pulley wheel was behind the clock mechanism.

Fortunately, the owner's clock repairman was coming to the house the next day to return another clock after servicing. I telephoned him and he assessed the damage advising me that it would not be too difficult for him to fix. Subsequently, having apologetically confessed my sin to the owner on his return, he very kindly didn't take up my offer to pay for the repair. I was certainly a lot more careful with clock winding subsequent to that episode and have even managed to fix a winding problem on my own regulator.

Video recorders presented a unique challenge. You might remember how long it took you to master the instructions for your own. I don't think we ever saw two the same in our travels and we have had a few cases where all our efforts to record a particular programme had met with failure, short of standing there and pressing record at the right time, particularly where we did not have any instructions. By the time we'd mastered a "new" machine, it was usually time to leave and the whole process started again on the next assignment.

Microwaves didn't seem to cause the same problems for Sue. Perhaps it was because she has also been a microwave demonstrator in her time.

Another long-term benefit of our house sitting career was to have the opportunity to try, and to evaluate, all manner of things without having first to purchase them. In addition to toasters, we include all kinds of kitchen appliances and gadgets, garden furniture, TVs and other electronic equipment in this category. We do subscribe to the most popular consumer magazine but there certainly is no substitute for hands-on experience and we formed some definite preferences from our experiences along the way.

We learned which vacuum cleaners actually picked up dog hairs and which ones just moved them about a bit. We also learned not to vacuum too near to an open fire. One of our owners had done just that and wondered why her cleaner caught fire soon afterwards. She had vacuumed around the sides and back of a wood burning stove and picked up some small, still glowing, embers. About ten minutes later the dust bag started to smoulder and we retain the humorous picture in our minds of her rushing out of the door carrying a burning vacuum cleaner. It might not have been so funny, however, if she had already put it away in the cupboard!

I was using the iron one day in one of our houses. You might say that real men don't do the ironing but ever since my apprentice days in the Royal Air Force I have insisted on ironing my own shirts and pressing my own trousers. Sue is all for it, as she hates ironing! There is a strong possibility that very early on in our relationship she accidentally on purpose did a poor job on some of my shirts. But we won't dwell on that topic here!

Anyway, in one house I turned round to Sue and said, "Someone in one of our other houses has this same iron."

"Yes," she said, - "**we** do!"

Just goes to show how many different irons we used around the country – or how much notice I took of them!

They say that you can always tell much about a person from the books he or she possesses. We can't truthfully say whether "they" are right but we did come across some varying and interesting libraries. We have quite a collection of books at home but we always looked forward to the chance to widen our horizons by browsing our hosts' bookshelves. It also saved carting library books around the country, which we often had to do!

I did not find a book on how to manage Rottweilers during that particular visit but I did read one on fly-casting before I ventured on to the trout lake. It didn't do me much good with my fishing but at least I might have looked the part! At least, to anyone who didn't fly- fish.

During our visits we did come across varying quantities of books. Everything from hundreds piled floor to ceiling, to none at all. One particular client, an author, possessed more books than our local library. There were one or two rooms which looked like the average home but the study, the attic, the landing, the edges of the stairs (three storeys), a storeroom beside the house and the large double garage were crammed full of thousands of volumes of all sizes and subject matter. I've never seen such a large private collection. We do hope that they never have to move house again!

Among the variety of animals/birds over which we have had charge were pheasants. Not one or two, but two thousand! Our owners had several large pens in their woodlands in which they were rearing young pheasants that would later be released for the annual "shoot". I'm not offering any opinions here about whether I am in favour of such a "sport" but let me just say I can think of far better things to do with my money and leisure time than to kill a few hundred relatively tame birds especially bred for the purpose.

Anyway, in the absence of the owner's wife, twice a day I had to visit three of the pens to top up their water and feed trays, check the fences and usher many escapees through special one-way tunnels back into their pens. There were lights to turn on and off to ward off owls at night and small electric fences to check. In all, the task took around half an hour and was quite pleasant on fine days. The early morning walk through the woods with the sunbeams filtering through the trees and the odd glimpse of a deer or a fox was invigorating. But on wet days, particularly after a long spell of rain, it became a chore slipping and sliding on muddy woodland paths with water dripping down my neck. Not a task you could put off until the rain stopped either. All in a day's work and very interesting to learn a little about these birds! I was glad however, that I did not have to look after all of the pens and that it was only for a couple of weeks not the whole six months it took to rear the poults to maturity.

Understandably, some people would schedule work to be carried out on their properties while they were away, I suppose to minimise the inconvenience. At one house it always seemed a coincidence that the septic tank would mysteriously require emptying soon after we arrived. In our notes, it would advertise the forthcoming event and the "honey wagon" would arrive on the appointed day. It would be parked at the front of the house, a huge hose would be run out through the side garden, across the lawn at the back, down to the tank at the bottom of the garden. Due to the length of hose involved, inevitably, there were several joints. Well, you can probably guess what I'm going to say next.

Sure enough, when the pumps started up the contents of the tank were slowly transferred to the truck with the inevitable oozing from the hose joints. We soon realised why this task was usually performed in the owners' absence. Despite the best efforts of the truck driver to clean up afterwards, the smell lingered for days! Of course, their dogs just loved to roll in the residue. What joy! Many hosings down and banishments from the house until dry.

At another house we counted eight other people coming and going during our stay. No, nine, I had forgotten the secretary who came to the house regularly to check the mail. There were three painters doing up the exterior of the house, two carpenters replacing an upstairs window, the gamekeeper and gardener who needed various keys from time to time and the cleaner. No rest for the wicked, we felt like we were in the middle of Piccadilly Circus!

It also seemed a smart move, on their part, to have several rooms re-carpeted in their absence. I can't really complain though as we have done the same! Far better to be out of the house whilst any major work is being carried out.

Lastly, on the topic of variety, we found it astonishing in how many different ways people controlled and fed their dogs. There seemed to be no distinct pattern.

Most owners had their own preferences for pet commands (pun intended) and we always made it a point to ask them for knowledge of these. "Stop" might work with one dog but not necessarily with another. Unfamiliar commands seldom work and can easily confuse a recently trained puppy. For example, "quick, quick," meant hurry up and water the lawn to one of our charges but would have been useless to any of the others.

One small dog cowered under the furniture when thunder rumbled or when a nearby army firing range was in use. It could only be pacified by the administration of homeopathic drops (named thunder drops by its owner) and reassurance with the words "stay with mummy," which we modified to read "me," instead of "mummy." The same dog had to have its biscuit at bedtime and after being covered in a blanket had to be told, "ni', ni'," so it would realise it was time to go to sleep. All in a day's work!

Instructions left for us regarding commands varied from none at all, through a brief verbal up-date to comprehensive written instructions, an example of which follows:

"Hello, my name is Alba and I'm coming to stay!! (Alba was the daughter's dog who came to stay at a house we were looking after whilst the daughter was away with her parents. You'll meet the dog of the house, Tatti, a little later on in the book.)

I'm only a puppy (nine months old) but I am learning very quickly and so far I know the following words/commands:

Sit	(treat over her nose)
Lie	(treat by her feet)
Off	(with a fist and treat) very useful with dishwasher etc.
Stand	(from sitting – treat in front)
Settle	(whenever she just lies down, give a treat and say good girl)
Come	(open arms, crouch down, big smile and a treat when she comes)
Good Girl	(as above)
No	(as above)
Look(	as above)
All Gone	(show empty hands)
This Way	(useful on walks when she goes off the wrong way)
Heel	(only just started to learn this)
Give a Paw	(she does this only for food or when she wants to)
Pfuii	(i.e. when she has her nose in manure etc – means smelly/bad)

Generally all good behaviour is rewarded (and I get lots of little treats throughout the day) and all bad behaviour is generally ignored except, of course, if I'm really bad, then I get a tap on my nose.

I am used to two walks a day – one in the morning before breakfast (half an hour) and one mid afternoon (one hour max). I love swimming and all water, but please check the current and any underwater obstacles first!

I'm still not very good on the lead and tend to sit still a lot, but I am getting better.

I eat two times a day (breakfast after morning walk and 5pm) – each meal is Nutro Puppy Choice and I get almost a full beaker (just under the blue line). If I'm lucky, a lunchtime biscuit.

My bedtime is generally around 10.30 – 11pm. I usually get my collar removed at bedtime, so that I can sleep soundly.

I love to chew cardboard boxes and old rolled up newspapers, but hopefully with Tatti I'll have a distraction. Mummy always gives me a rusk, biscuit ball, marmite or cube when she goes out so that I'm distracted.

I love going to the vets, as I get lots of attention and treats. I am fully up to date on all my injections, flea spot-on and worming (as you can see from my record); my vet details are: (address supplied)

I am terrified of hot air balloons, fireworks and people flying kites! I tend to shake a lot and then run away.

I recently got attacked by two Staffordshire Bull Terriers, it was a vicious attack and they bit my bottom badly and near my tail on the right hand side. Although I still love Tatti it has made me a little cautious of other dogs. But I'm learning again to trust.

The only other thing is that I might come on heat as I'm nine months old!!

Thank you for looking after me – I hope that I'll be a good girl. xxx

How cute! The dog was as well, and she was really well behaved for a nine-month old golden retriever.

Alba

****

We often received copious written instructions. Quite understandable really, and we soon created a comprehensive standard check list of our own for all the essential information that we required to run the houses and look after pets in the manner to which they were accustomed. Instructions ranged from a hastily written few words on scraps of paper to computer generated, well organised lists of every aspect of information you could imagine might be necessary.

However, we drew the line with one of our regular owners when they felt it necessary to write down that we, "should keep (XXXX) on a tight short lead if walking on the pavement as she tended to chase traffic."

By then we had been looking after their dogs for about five years and we felt it a little more than unnecessary to remind us of that basic fact. We're not sure who was more neurotic, the dog or the owners. They had always been more of the worrying kind than most of our owners. On our last visit there we had a telephone call every day from southern Europe. So we "fired" them and never went back. Shame really, as it was a delightful house in a lovely village!

Many owners were concerned that their pets would pine in their absence, would miss them and go off their food. Not a bit of it! Although dogs do seem to know what suitcases are for and would often mope around in their presence, especially if the luggage was parked by the front door ready for departure. However, the vast majority would stare at the retreating car or taxi for a minute or two and then see what mischief they could get up to with us. I don't think we ever had one dog that wouldn't eat its regular ration and still come back for more.

As far as missing their owners was concerned, we even had one dog whose people had been away for two months make a great fuss of the taxi driver on their return. She completely ignored her owners, much to their embarrassment and annoyance!

Some owners fed their pets once, some twice and some three times a day with varying types and quantities of food and not just relative to their pets' ages or size. Whether they were puppies or fully grown, it did not seem to matter. Types of food varied greatly, of course, but so did the timing, whether it was hot or cold, wet or dry, with or without vegetables, even one vegetarian, and many more variations.

We were always pleased to see that the great majority of dogs did not get cake, biscuits, chocolate or sweets and, of course, we always treated them all as their owners would. How Fisky our spaniel survived his massive intake of Easter chocolate all those years ago in Devon, we'll never know.

We did see some dogs on our travels, however, that were clearly overfed and overweight although, thankfully, not any of those over which we had charge.

In her time, my sister had looked after two Labradors that could have doubled as coffee tables they were so obese. Several cups and saucers would have balanced perfectly well on their flat backs! It is a shame that this misplaced kindness can result in an early demise and we wish more people would realise that, as with humans, there is no substitute for a sensible diet and plenty of exercise. One of those two Labradors has since died at an early age and we attributed this directly to overfeeding.

Chapter Eight

Cats (And Other Things)

The astute reader will be aware that cats have not figured much so far in these pages. This is not because we do not like cats as much as dogs, or that cats were necessarily in the minority in the households we visited. More so that cats, being the independent types that they are, did not tend to be with us as much as their canine companions and therefore did not present us with nearly as many humorous or interesting situations. Sue you may remember had a cat when we met, but it made the decision to stay with a neighbour when we moved to Devon.

One "cat"astrophe does rate a mention and it was on another of Sue's solo assignments. In her care Sue had my sister's large golden retriever called Toby, a chocolate lab named Emma and an ailing, aged cat called Tabitha. Sebastian, her farmyard poodle (remember him?) was also with her.

It was early on a winter's morning, the rain was persisting down, and it was time to let the dogs out for their morning "ablutions". Sue, barely awake, came bare-footed down the stairs, dressed only in a kaftan, went into the kitchen and closed the door behind her to be greeted by three equally sleepy dogs. She spotted Tabitha on a shelf and decided that the cat would be better off in her bed on top of a radiator. Having first positioned Tabitha's bed, Sue picked up the cat, whereupon it carefully stretched out its paws and inserted one of its claws into her nose and through the fleshy part of the septum! For the medically challenged that is the extremely tender bit between the two nostrils! I only learned that because of this event.

By this time all the dogs were wide-awake and clamouring to go out. If you own a dog, or have ever had one, you'll know how demonstrably keen they are to get out of the door first thing in the morning. Or for any walk, for that matter!

Sue now had her hands full with the cat, not a lightweight by any means, and her efforts to dislodge the claw from her nose only made matters worse. The claw was embedded at such an angle that no movement Sue could make would free it, without great pain. She tried in vain to find a mirror to help see what she was doing. There wasn't one in the kitchen and the glass door of the built-in oven did not provide enough of a reflection to be of any use. The door handle back into the remainder of the house was of the round knob type and Sue could not get enough purchase on it whilst keeping poor old Tabitha's weight from pulling at her nose.

The dogs were barking and jumping up, after a night indoors, and there was no one Sue could turn to for help. Both hands were needed to support the weight of the cat, phoning was out of the question and the nearest neighbours were across the lane about five hundred yards distant down a very muddy drive. What was worse, that neighbour owned a bulldog of dubious character: i.e. of an unknown tolerance towards cats.

Considering all the options, there was only one course of action - Sue had to enlist the help of the neighbour. Remember that she was barefoot, it was raining hard, she was clad in only a kaftan and had no hands. First, there were the feet to consider. Her wellies were by the back door and were the only footwear (on hand, so to speak) on her only possible exit route.

Now, opening doors is easy if you have two hands free, or at least one. But when you are delicately trying to support a cat at nose level, fortunately not wriggling too much, with a claw in your left nostril ("cat up your nose," as Sue often calls it when relating the story) it becomes no mean feat. Down on her knees, surrounded by agitated dogs, who thought it was all a huge game, she managed to unlock the back door with two fingers and turned the lever-type handle without letting go of the cat. Even if Sue wasn't, the dogs, at least, were now free.

She had finally made it to the wellies. Now, have you ever tried to put on a pair of pliable long rubber boots when not wearing socks and without using your hands? You haven't? Well, it's not easy. Take Sue's word for it! In fact it is almost impossible, especially if they are a tight fit in the first place.

The inevitable happened. Sue's feet became stuck halfway down each boot, so she was now standing there with the boots half on and the bottom half of the wellies sticking out at the sides. However, always fashion conscious, Sue was pleased to note that the blue, sequined kaftan went exceedingly well with her duck-feet dark blue wellies.

The next stage must have looked the most amusing, with hindsight, of course, as Sue was now waddling down the garden in the pouring rain, wellies flapping sideways, cat in arms in search of a knight in shining armour. She crossed the lane, fortunately not a busy thoroughfare, particularly at that time of the morning and started down the neighbour's drive, squelching noisily in the mud.

Across the road they had the builders in and their drive was a quagmire. At any moment she was expecting the bulldog to appear. Fortunately, the son of the house, being a sensible type, on seeing a soaking wet, kaftan-clad, wellie flapping lady with a cat up her nose and tears in her eyes coming down the drive, realised something might be slightly amiss and had the presence of mind to keep the bulldog in the house.

By now Sue's hair was wringing wet, her nose and eyes were running and she was well beyond the "good morning, pity about the weather, how are you?" stage. Anyway, no words were needed, as the situation must have appeared pretty obvious. Between them, and with great care, Sue and the neighbour eventually managed to dislodge the cat and order was restored to an otherwise tranquil country scene.

The sad sequel to the story is that the cat died two days after my sister's return. Not from its experience with Sue, I hasten to add. It was on its last legs anyway. During her stay Sue had contacted the vet about the cat's near comatose condition (well before the "cat up the nose" episode) and the vet's recommendation had been to have it put down. However, quite rightly, he had also advised that the owners should make that decision as the cat was in no pain. I was quite glad that that was the case, as Raine would not have been very pleased if we had taken that decision.

****

You might appreciate that during our own dog owning years and on our various assignments we had a fair bit to do with the veterinary profession. Over the years we got to know some vets quite well and I must relate one tale that we heard. However, I dare not tell you even in which county the following was said to have happened.

A customer had brought the family cat in to the vet and as it was so old and poorly there was no other option than to have it put down. This was done and the unhappy lady left for home. As was the normal practice the vet put the now deceased cat in the "small animal" freezer to await collection by the appropriate disposal contractor.

However, early the next morning he received a telephone call from the cat's owner saying that her small daughter was still very upset about the cat's demise. To soften the blow the lady felt sure that the daughter would benefit from seeing the poor animal in its restful state. She would then understand the nature of things, realise that the cat was no longer suffering and had met a painless and peaceful end to its life.

Of course, by this time, the cat was frozen solid. But the vet, being a kind and thoughtful sort, as most vets are, reassured the lady that it would be alright to bring her daughter into the surgery later that morning to see her beloved pet.

There followed frantic scenes while the staff retrieved the cat from the freezer, thawed it out as best they could with the aid of a hair dryer and generally tried to tidy it up to look as near as possible to how it did when it was alive. The poor thing had just been put in the freezer any old how, limbs were sticking out in all directions and its tongue was protruding through its teeth! Amid much, perhaps irreverent, but maybe understandable, hilarity they eventually restored the cat to a presentable condition, combed its coat and adjusted its facial expression to reflect an expression of perfect peace.

Final preparations were concluded just in time for the visit of the bereaved little girl. She spent a few minutes with her beloved cat and left, reassured that her pet was in no pain. Both the mother and the veterinary staff breathed sighs of relief, but for very different reasons!

In all of our time looking after other people's pets we had very few occasions where we needed to take one to the vet. One such dog was Noodle, a sixteen-year-old spaniel who caught one of her claws on something and although not in a great deal of pain, it just would not heal despite our first aid treatment. We trundled her off to the local vet and were amazed to find that the same girl who had been our vet, and my sister's, some years previously at Biggin Hill in Kent was working in the practice in Forest Row in East Sussex. Even more of a coincidence was that my sister who had also moved to East Sussex was now using the same surgery. Roxanne, the vet, was originally from New Zealand. Have you ever noticed that nearly all vets are from either the Antipodes or Scotland? There must be something in the water.

****

I mentioned earlier that at least one place we have looked after kept doves. Quite a few places had dovecotes in fact. My sister also had some, which she fed and watered every day. Her collection started out mostly pure white with a few beautiful brown and white doves with ruffs at their necks. Over time the doves obviously played away from home and gradually their colouring evened out and she was left with only two pure white doves. The rest comprised of a mixture of brown, black and white.

Feeding Time

Some people went to great lengths to keep their birds pure bred. The most drastic, and somewhat cruel we thought, was to shoot any that appeared in addition to, or instead of, members of their original flock. However, if you are used to shooting pheasant or grouse as a sport, then I guess a few pigeons would not cause you to lose any sleep. After all, in medieval times dove or pigeon-cotes were built to provide a self- replenishing source of food. However, I don't think I could shoot doves or pigeons but I must admit I've been tempted to shoot at the odd crow or two when I have found pieces of dead doves under my sister's dove-cote. Magpies and pigeons are a different kettle of fish, so to speak, and I am not against shooting these birds if it means other birds and/or garden vegetables are to survive.

One couple we know hit upon another, much more humane way to purify their flock. Easy, they thought, we'll just round up the misfits, put them in a basket and set them free many miles from home. They lived in East Sussex and were due to take a trip to the wilds of Norfolk. In case anyone from Norfolk takes offence at my description, yes, I have spent a lot of time in that county and parts of it are wild. At least, the traditional jazz clubs in Norwich were when I was there in the heady mid-sixties! A fine city!

Anyway, the birds were collected, placed in a basket and were taken to Norfolk where they were released in dense woodland. Their owners set off for their journey home satisfied in the knowledge that they had done the right thing. Lives had been spared and their flock once again would consist of pure white birds. You've probably guessed what happened next. Yes, when our nature loving owners arrived home their birds were waiting for them looking so pleased that they had found their way home and beaten their owners to it as well. If birds could be said to be laughing, their owner told us they were!

I never found out what happened subsequently but I hope the returnees were allowed to stay!

****

We often received telephone calls from people after they had left, on mobile phones, from airports, hotels or wherever. Usually they wanted to let us know about something they had omitted to tell us before leaving; rubbish day, window cleaner; that sort of thing.

Perhaps the strangest was the call we received from the departing owners at an airport, which advised us that before they left they had not been able to find their cat. On thinking about it, on the way to the airport the lady of the house had recalled that she had been into the loft just before leaving and she was worried that the cat may have followed her up there.

We went up the stairs, opened up the loft hatch, let down the ladder and called the cat. No response. Of course the cat did not know us and would not therefore necessarily respond to a strange voice. There was nothing else for it but to climb the ladder and explore the roof space. Sure enough, there he was and he eventually allowed himself to be "rescued". Had we not had the telephone call it might have remained there for some time as we were not actually staying at that particular house, only visiting twice a day and there was therefore no real need to go upstairs.

It was at that house that we looked after perhaps our oddest combination of pets. Along with the cat there was an internal/external aviary with a number of parakeets and two budgerigars and a series of ponds with somewhere between thirty and forty Koi carp. There were also several other small fish in tanks and another pond. They all obviously lived happily together and we had no problems during our time with them.

Our morning visits entailed opening up the aviary, checking the birds' food and water and carrying one elderly budgerigar (Tommy) in its cage from inside the house to the aviary. Here he spent the day, still in his cage, but able to talk to the other "free flying" budgie. The cat had to be fed and then there were the fish! The smallest Koi must have been about twelve inches long but the largest was all of two feet six inches! They were housed in two large interconnected ponds kept at a constant temperature and cleanliness by a special heater and filtration system.

After feeding, there were the filters to check and clean, involving a detailed sequence of operating pumps, switches and cocks. Not much fun when it was raining and chilly, as I had to lift heavy wooden covers and climb down into a pit to carry out this task. Next, the water temperature had to be checked and adjusted and the smaller fish also had to be fed. Finally, if it was to be a sunny day, a cover was to be rigged above one of the ponds. We had not realised until then that fish can get sunburnt!

In the evening, roughly the reverse procedure had to be followed. The "free" budgie was sometimes difficult to catch but most of the parakeets would go into the internal side of the aviary without needing too much persuasion.

We were relieved that the owners returned to find that all was well with our various charges, particularly as we knew that the fish were of considerable value.

****

Turning the clock back to the time Sue and I first met in Yorkshire, she also had a large cat named Sylvester, in addition to Sebbie the poodle. Sylvester was one of those independent creatures that thought he didn't really belong to anyone and came and went as he pleased – bit like most cats really. He was never very happy with other dogs, except Sebbie, and Jason had just passed on before we moved in together. We had not acquired Spey before we left Yorkshire for Devon. On our departure from Yorkshire we left Sylvester with a neighbour of Sue's, to whom the cat had become more attached than to Sue. So, fortunately, we were cat-less when Spey eventually took up residence with us in our cottage in Devon.

There was one really memorable moment in Sylvester's life that warrants recording here. At the time Sue lived in a second floor flat in a U shaped "luxury executive apartment" block with garages and storerooms on the ground floor, underneath the first floor flats. In the centre of the U was a square lawn, maybe about fifty yards across with ornate flowerbeds and shrubs dotted about. The flat was in Wetherby, Yorkshire and I was away on a business trip to Scotland. It was very late at night and most people were asleep in bed.

Suddenly, there was a huge explosion that echoed round the quadrangle - then a series of smaller explosions. They were loud enough to wake Sue, and that's saying something. She leapt out of bed and peered out of the window. Lights were coming on and heads were appearing from other windows all around the complex but there was nothing to be seen.

Eventually, peace returned, heads withdrew and Sue went back to bed. She was just dozing off again when she suddenly remembered the homemade elderflower champagne and ginger beer in the storeroom two floors below. She knew instantly what had happened but, more importantly, and significantly, she remembered with increasing dread that Sylvester used the storeroom as his bedroom on the frequent occasions that he spent the night on the tiles. This was such a night and Sue had a mental picture of a fragmented Sylvester covering the ceiling among the glass and contents of several bottles of elderflower champagne and ginger beer.

Unwilling to reconnoitre alone at that time of night, particularly with the potential gory sight in the room below, she telephoned her downstairs neighbour for moral and physical support.

"Did you hear that explosion?" Sue said.

"Not only did I hear it," her neighbour replied, "it lifted my bed off the floor."

Sue anxiously related her fears and the neighbour reluctantly agreed to accompany her downstairs to survey the scene. They gingerly (ha!) opened the storeroom door to be greeted by a sweet sickly smell and the sight of the floor, walls and ceiling covered in various layers of goo that had been the ginger beer and elderflower champagne. Fortunately, there appeared to be no bits of cat among the debris. The force of the blast had been such that several cases had exploded in a chain reaction and pieces of glass and bottle tops were actually embedded in the concrete ceiling.

Satisfied that Sylvester had not been involved, Sue and her neighbour returned to their respective flats and Sue just had to telephone me to tell me the story. I was not best pleased about being woken at zero dark thirty in the morning to hear of Sylvester's miraculous escape but we do still smile when we think about the scene that night in that exclusive, hitherto quiet, respectable neighbourhood.

A couple of months before the explosion episode Sue and I took Sebbie and Jason up to Scotland to visit some friends near Aviemore and stopped for a picnic lunch on the way, somewhere well into the Scottish hills. When we were travelling and we stopped to eat, or even just for a break, we always sought to get off the motorways or main roads and find a quiet spot with a decent view, away from the noise and fumes of the traffic.

To this day it amazes us how many people we see eating their sandwiches, or brewing tea, sitting in lay-bys on main roads with traffic thundering past. They never seem to appreciate that, for a few miles extra effort, there are countless places where their sojourn would be far more pleasant.

Anyway, this particular day we drove about two miles off the main road, opened an unlocked gate leading into a large field, settled down and started our lunch. The field stretched far away over the brow on the side of a hill with a glorious view down the valley and, as we could not see any sheep or cattle, we let the dogs run free.

All was well for a while. We had almost finished our meal when Jason let out a strangled yelp. He jumped about three feet into the air with his coat standing on end, hurtled towards the gate, which he cleared with ease, and then ran as fast as he could along a lane and disappeared out of sight. We were mystified. I ran back to the car, jumped in and set off up the hill in pursuit hoping that Jason would remain on the road and not take it into his head to veer off across country. I saw him in the distance, caught up and managed to overtake him, then stopped the car some distance up the lane. On seeing me he calmed down a little, came to a halt and I managed to get him into the car although he was still trembling with very evident and severe fright.

It was only on the way back down to our picnic site, having a better field of view due to the rise in the land that I saw a huge nasty-looking black bull just over the brow of the hill from where we had been sitting. I realised that the bull had only been about a hundred yards from where we had been having our picnic and only the contour of the field had prevented us from seeing him, or he us!

I left Jason in the car, tip-toed through the gate, whispered the news of our potentially dangerous neighbour to Sue and we hastily, but quietly, packed up our kit, collected Sebbie and left the scene as quickly as possible. No, Jason had not been frightened or attacked by the bull but had received a shock from the electric fence, which we had not even noticed!

Apparently, in that area although strictly against the law it was fairly common practice to wire electric fences to the mains. We found this out on asking a passer-by and we then realised that Jason had survived a 240 volts shock! Thankfully, Sebbie was too short to reach the electrified strands but we realised that we ourselves had also been at great risk - and not only from the bull!

Later, we felt that we should have brought this to the attention of the local authorities but we continued on our journey shaken, but much wiser about one of the lesser known and more dangerous country practices. If that particular farmer ever reads this I hope he realises that he could have killed someone that day. Incidentally, not only was there no notice posted about the electric fence but the bull's presence was similarly unannounced.

Jason seemed none the worse for his ordeal, although I did wonder whether the strokes he suffered some time later, prior to his death, were as a result of this unfortunate experience.

****

You might have gathered that most of "our" houses were located in very rural settings. Our own place in Harrogate, North Yorkshire backs on to the famous Stray. Famous that is, if you have ever heard of it! Close to the town centre there is a two hundred acre L shaped area of grass that the Duchy of Lancaster in the early 1800s, gave to the citizens of the town in perpetuity for recreational purposes and it provides a pleasant oasis of quiet between us and the rest of the town. We therefore have the benefit of being able to walk into our picturesque spa town across the Stray, yet we retain a quiet rural atmosphere.

However, in the even more rural locations enjoyed by the owners of the houses we looked after, and therefore much enjoyed by ourselves on occasion, there were as you might imagine pros and cons to be found at each different site. Accepting that isolation and plenty of space gives one privacy and a feeling of comfort, mostly peace and quiet, and a feeling of well-being, there are also a few minuses along the way.

Regrettably these days, security is an important factor when considering purchase of a house in the country. All of the houses we looked after had dogs on the premises and one of the main reasons for their owners not wishing to place their pets in kennels during their absence was, of course, security. Dogs can be a very effective deterrent to the potential thief. During a three year appointment in

Zambia many years ago we kept an Alsation in the house. It was no coincidence that houses all around us were broken into on a regular basis but we remained untouched.

I recall a letter in the Daily Telegraph recently in which the correspondent was commenting on previous letters about the vulnerability of country houses after a spate of break-ins. He wrote, "My wife and I have lived in our isolated house in the country for many years without any problems. We just cannot understand what your previous correspondents are talking about - and neither can our two Alsations!"

Of course, a good intruder alarm system preferably connected to the police or a security company is another must, as is an efficient security lighting system. Regrettably, such systems are the price to pay these days for peace of mind, personal safety and security of one's possessions, particularly regarding isolated properties.

We saw a marked difference in people's attitude to security. Some owners didn't give it much thought, whilst others took every precaution possible. One owner told us that they had been burgled three times but he still did not lock his garage or garden shed – even at night! Strange when garden machinery and tools are currently much sought after by the criminal fraternity. Another owner actually had a wheel clamp fitted to his ride-on mower, even though it was padlocked inside a garage. Some people had sophisticated alarm systems but did not always set them. We always set ours at home before leaving and, even in residence, when we retire for the night by using the partial set facility.

Similarly, it is surprising the number of people who still leave spare keys in far too obvious places outside the house. None of our owners left keys under the door mat but any potential thief would not have too much trouble locating keys under plant pots, stones and the like, close to the front or back doors. For goodness sake people! If you must leave keys outside for emergency access, and it's not such a bad idea to do so, put them as far away from the house as you can and in a much less obvious position. The further away from the building you can hide a key the wider the search area for the bad guys. And, for pity's sake, do not hide them in the garage!

Leaving a set of keys with a neighbour or two has its benefits as well. Three times I managed to lock myself out of other people's houses but fortunately two of them had keys deposited with neighbours. The third was a little different.

At this particular house, we had an elaborate departure routine when walking the dogs as they had to go out of the back French windows which then had to be triple locked – from the inside. Once outside, the dogs were left in the garage while I went back through the house locking the French windows. Then, I left the house through the front door getting my boots and the dogs from the front door of the garage.

Fine so far on this particular occasion. On my way out of the front door I left it open. Having collected my boots, before putting them on, I went back inside to set the burglar alarm. I had just punched in the numbers when one of the dogs ran in through the front door and disappeared down the hall. By now the alarm is giving me the "hurry up and leave or we'll call the cops, signal" and it took me quite a while to collar the dog, shepherd it through the door and to slam it behind me. Just made it!

Ah! I thought. The key is on the chest just inside the front door! You do feel such a fool in these circumstances.

Now that morning for the first time ever during our stay I had closed the little window in the upstairs bedroom we were using. I don't know why, I just did. It would have been a simple task to get the long ladders out of the garage, climb up, open the small window, release the latch on the bigger window and gain entry. I reckon I could have made downstairs and neutralized the alarm before it called the sheriff. But, all that was not now possible.

Anyway, the dogs were anxious for their walk and there was no need for immediate action. The house was secure, huh! So we took the dogs for their walk and spent the time devising a plan of action. Simple, we thought, just break that small window, get in the same way and all would be fine. Barring us having to pay the glazier's bill.

Then we had another idea. Adjacent to the house was a small cottage and we had noticed that there was new putty in one of the glass panes of its back door. As the internal door between the house and the cottage was normally left open perhaps we could gain access that way. Sure enough, when we got back it was relatively easy to carefully remove the still moist putty, ease the pane of glass out and, with some difficulty, squeeze through the opening.

Once inside, I reached the connecting door only to find that it had been bolted from the other side, presumably by the cleaner who had been just the day before. Foiled again.

However, all was not lost. We remembered that the main house utility room window was always left open, albeit there was a steel bar fixed horizontally across the opening to deter people such as us in using that avenue of entry. Time to call in reinforcements. My sister lived only a short distance away and we called her – thank the Lord for mobile phones – to ask her if she could come over and bring a hacksaw. The hacksaw duly arrived and we made short work of the bar, which allowed the slimmest of us, I can't tell you who it was, to clamber through and let us in.

Lest you think we caused permanent damage to the premises let me assure you that my brother-in-law has a workshop, of which even the Ferrari motor racing team would be proud. Well, nearly. It was therefore relatively easy, a little later, to arc weld the offending bar and after a coat of paint all was restored to its former glory.

From that day it became standard policy – always keep door keys in one's coat pocket. Fine in the winter but on summer days we were back to ensuring that keys were always with us before shutting doors. A set of keys well hidden outside or lodged with a neighbour is, without doubt, a much better back-up plan.

Worryingly, many of "our" houses did not have smoke alarms installed. A definite must, particularly in older houses with venerable electrical wiring and, often, wooden panelling and/or beamed ceilings. Many insurance companies will not insure older houses these days without adequate fire or smoke detectors being in place. With all the publicity given to crime statistics, particularly in rural areas, it was also surprising to us how many country houses with relatively insecure doors and windows still did not have alarm systems.

****

Talking of windows, we loved this tale one of our owners told us. She had been concerned about the standard of work of her window cleaner so she decided to set him a little trap. On the day of the cleaner's next visit she placed a £1 coin on one of the least accessible window sills. Come settling up time she gave him the usual amount less £1 and the window cleaner asked why he was not being paid the full amount.

She told him about the coin on the window ledge and he admitted that he had missed that one window on this occasion and apologised profusely. To keep the window cleaner on his toes in the future she subsequently placed coins to the full amount of his fee on window sills all over the house to ensure that the cleaner got to every window!

This was also the lady who previously had asked the same window cleaner whether he had ever been in the navy.

He looked puzzled and said, "No, what makes you ask that?"

She pointed to the dirt in the corners of her windows and replied, "It looks like you have been used to cleaning portholes."

****

Same lady, completely different situation. She had been involved in a car crash and had suffered whiplash over which she had sued the other driver for compensation. At the subsequent court hearing the opposition's lawyer was conducting his cross-examination.

"Madam, since the accident have you managed to do your housework?"

Now Mrs X, who had only recently been widowed, had not actually done any housework to speak of for years. So she said, "Well no actually but I do get someone in to do it for me."

The lawyer was unfazed by this and came back with, "Well, can you still do gardening?"

Mrs X had not been particularly active in the garden over the years either so she quite truthfully said, again, "No but I get a man in to do that for me."

Inevitably the lawyer had to ask about her sex life and inquired whether the accident had affected her in that area. Before she could reply, the lawyer started to say, somewhat sarcastically, "I suppose you….." But at least he had the decency not to complete the sentence.

****

By far the largest animals we have had in our care were five bullocks belonging to the son of one of our owners. The young but already huge beasts were grazing in fields adjacent to the house that we were looking after. Now, I must be honest and tell you that all we had to do was count them each day. That is, only to check that they were safe, upright and breathing. There was plenty of grass upon which they could graze in two large fields and they had access to a stream running through the property so there were no problems with feeding etc. Our house owner was a retired farmer and his son, who was also a farmer, occasionally used his father's paddocks for additional grazing.

My excuse for mentioning the cattle here is that come round-up time we had some hairy moments getting these young beasts out of the field into the lorry. We had helped out with herding cows before with very little effort, or problems. On this occasion the owner's son had telephoned to say he would be coming round to collect the cattle and we had decided to offer our assistance.

Now, I have a lot of respect for big dogs but I have a whole lot more for large, scared, skittish cattle - especially bullocks. We had little trouble getting them to the gate in the corner of the field but from there they had to climb a hill up a lane, round a corner, through another gate down another lane, the owner's drive, and up the ramp into their lorry. Sounds easy!

The trouble was that leading off the lanes were other outlets, without gates, allowing access to the rest of the garden. As a precaution we had assembled various obstacles including an old car, a wheel- barrow and a garden bench to deter the cattle from deviating from the desired path and we felt pretty confident that all would be well.

It all started off perfectly. The cattle allowed themselves to be herded out of the field quite easily and very little effort was required to get them up the first bit of lane but they baulked at going through the second gate. By this time we had closed the gate behind us, which led back into the field. All our efforts failed to get them through the second gate and the cattle were getting more and more agitated. Suddenly, they about-turned and we scattered.

Discretion has always been, in my book, the better part of valour. Besides, what the heck was I doing at fifty-several years old risking my neck playing at cowboys? Thankfully, there were ample stout trees behind which we took cover as they lumbered by. Two of the bullocks ran back down the lane, clambered up a bank and jumped a wire fence next to the gate and ended up back in the field. The other three surged through a narrow opening in a wall that we had not seen fit to block and headed off towards the rose and vegetable garden.

We split our forces (there were four of us) and between us we herded the beasts back out of the field, closed the gate, extricated the others out of the garden, blocked the narrow opening with an old door and headed them back up the lane. Again, it might sound easy on paper but by this time we were sweating and breathing somewhat faster than normal. The cattle were more than a little excited and there were deep hoof prints and other deposits that cattle tend to leave behind, especially when they are excited, on the lawns and drive. Thankfully, no damage had been done to the rest of the garden apart from the aforesaid hoof prints and copious biodegradable nutrient-rich heaps.

Fortunately, the bullocks went through the second gate this time with very little effort, on their part that is, not ours, but could we get them to climb the ramp into their wagon? No, we could not and we had several anxious moments when they wheeled about and threatened to flatten us against the walls of the lane. Twice we had to let them run by and wait a respectable time whilst they, and we, calmed down again. It was beginning to feel a bit like snakes and ladders. At least by this time we had secured all possible means of escape apart from the ramp into the lorry so, thankfully, we did not have to go right back to square one.

Eventually we made enough noise with old plastic fertilizer bags (Sue's idea!) and through the scientific application of those old farmers' tools, a stout stick or two, we managed to get the beasts into the lorry.

I was glad I never had to do that for a living!

Same owner, but at a different house, we were asked to check on some new-born calves every day. Not just that they were all there and looking healthy but we were to inspect their droppings to see if the colour and consistency was normal! Well! I know you can tell a lot from excrement but I didn't happen to be an expert! However, I received a thorough briefing on colours, texture and the dangers of new calves eating too much green grass and I became an instant authority on cow shit!

Lest you think I spent the next two weeks peering at cow pats I must disappoint you. As there was a bull in the same field, together with some very offspring-protective cows, my observations were carried out at relatively long range and always behind the cover of a barbed wire fence.

Back to the far more pleasant subject of cats, I must record here a story that actually happened a few years back, in England, during a strike by the Fire Service. The Army had been called in to handle fires and other emergencies and was using old, but still functioning fire engines called Green Goddesses. One afternoon a call was received from a little old lady advising that her cat was stuck up a tall tree just outside her house.

"Could the army please come and rescue it?"

"Of course, the army would be delighted to assist."

Good public relations had always been their policy and here was an ideal way to put it into effect and relieve the boredom of a long spell of uneventful duty.

The Green Goddess duly arrived, parked in the old lady's drive and one of the army crew scaled a ladder with relative ease and brought the cat down safely to its owner. She was delighted, thanked them profusely and invited the crew in for tea and cakes. They gladly accepted her offer and after gratefully partaking of her kind hospitality they jumped into their fire engine, backed out and, unfortunately, ran over the cat, killing it instantly.

Of course, it was nobody's fault but the poor lady was so upset, as were the hapless crew.

I tell that story here not because it has a great deal of sadness attached to what should have been a happy ending. It may even, to the more macabre, have a doubtfully funny side to it. Hopefully though, it might remind us all to check behind and under our vehicles before reversing.

Similar things have happened to small children.

****

One of the nicest cats we met was a very small, but perfectly formed, male called Buthead. Apparently named after Bevis and Buthead, the American cartoon series but Bevis had met his end sometime previously at the hands of a careless driver. Buthead was an outside cat, as he did not get on with one of the spaniels in the house. Well, it was really the other way round but he was so friendly and always pleased to see us. He even followed us, at a discreet distance, on many of our long walks through the woods and fields on their owner's property, together with the three spaniels of the house and Arnie, a grand old golden retriever.

Buthead

****

I spent three years of my Royal Air Force career fighting the cold war. Not 'The' Cold War, you understand, although I guess I must have played a small part in that one way or another. No, I was really fighting the cold whilst working in MOD offices in Harrogate, North Yorkshire. A set of buildings built as a hospital for temporary use during World War Two was still in use as Government offices some thirty five years later together with the original iron frame windows (no double glazing) single brick walls and no insulation. Consequently, we froze in the winter and boiled in the summer. Like all good civil service establishments the central heating switch on and switch off dates were arbitrarily dictated by the calendar and did not take any account of the actual temperatures.

However, locked in my memory though that is, it's not the story here. The establishment was guarded by the Ministry of Defence Police, affectionately known as mod plods. They were mainly ex-servicemen or ex-policemen, many in their later years, and some did seem to relish the authority and over-estimate their importance in the whole scheme of things. Security was far less important then, than it is now with all the ramifications of global terrorism. Vital though our task was, I doubt we would have figured high on anyone's hit list but we did have to show our passes to get into the office and there were forms in triplicate to be completed if someone dared visit, or a security pass had been left at home.

I didn't live too far away from the office, well within easy walking distance in fact, which was great as I still had Jason (remember him?) with me at the time and I could walk him every lunch-time.

One of my near neighbours had a cat that was prone to wander, and it often refused its food on returning home. It was pretty obvious that wherever the cat was going someone was feeding it. This went on for several weeks until one day, the cat's owner noticed something around its neck when it returned after one of its wanderings.

On examination, the cat had been issued with an MOD pass, complete with photograph, to enter our buildings. I had often seen a cat wandering around the site but had not connected it with my neighbour's cat.

Who said policemen don't have a sense of humour? It was good to see that a regular visitor to our office had been afforded the proper documentation. It must have been hell each time, previously, for it to have filled in all those forms in triplicate!

Chapter Nine

A Spanish Interlude

Between "jobs" one year we took a long road trip through France and Spain to see parts of those countries "which other tourists cannot reach". The only reservations we made were for the ferries at either end of our journey, which was to last twenty eight days and took us down the western side of France and Spain to Gibraltar and then back up the Mediterranean coast and across France to Cherbourg.

The trip holds many memories but I'll skip over the stories of hotels in France with cardboard walls, bathrooms in cupboards and hall lights that are timed to go out just as you reach your room door but have not yet found the key hole! I'll stick to a story loosely associated with the theme of this book, i.e. pets, particularly dogs.

We had been travelling all day somewhere in the back and beyond of Andalucia and the time was fast approaching when we had to find somewhere to stay the night. Moron de la Frontera was the next town on the map and the road beyond was described as mountainous, picturesque but "dangerous at night" so we decided that this was as far as we should go that evening.

We approached the town looking for suitable accommodation but apart from the odd hostel or two we saw nothing we thought would suit us. Darkness was almost upon us so we stopped at a police station to test our Spanish on the local constabulary. In my best (school boy) Spanish I enquired about hotels but it was pretty obvious that I was not getting through to the man behind the desk as the only response I received was a shrug of the shoulders, a "que?" or two and rapid-fire Spanish in response. Come to think of it, he did look a bit like Manuel from Fawlty Towers!

My limited lingual expertise could not cope with this and we were getting nowhere. Suddenly, the man disappeared into an inner office and, after a few minutes, he, or his twin brother, re-emerged and we started again. I expected to see Basil or Sybil appear any moment. Had we been in a hotel, I would certainly have expected to see them.

"Nosotros quieremos accommodation por esta noche, por favor," I said. (Those among you who are Spanish linguists will immediately be aware of my limitations)

To our surprise he replied, in near perfect English.

"There is a nice motel just outside of town about three kilometres down the road."

I can only guess that my Spanish was so bad that he must have thought that we were from Belgium, Mesopotamia or worse. We expressed our "muchas graciases" and left, armed with our information. On the way out of the police station we noticed a certificate of appreciation from the United States Air Force, a small part of which occupied a huge air base close to the town.

Without too much trouble we found the motel, which looked great at that time of evening and we pulled in to the reception area. Sitting on the front door steps were two good looking girls in tight tank tops almost hiding their copious shapely contents, together with mini skirts that nearly did the same for their legs. Nice place, I thought. Of course, Sue was more attracted to the delightful little poodle puppy playing around the girls.

The girls spoke reasonable English and, yes, they had a room that although not in the Savoy or Ritz league was clean, air-conditioned and well within our budget.

Suitcases were unloaded and we next sought to attend to our usual priorities when stopping for the night. A cold beer, a hot shower then food and wine - invariably in that order. The hotel had a fully stocked bar in the foyer but, on asking, the girls told me that the hotel bar was closed but that the petrol station across the road had a bar! I asked what time the restaurant opened and was amazed to hear that it also was closed. Here we were in a large two storey motel with all the amenities and no bar or restaurant service. It wasn't even the off season but they seemed to be off!

Meanwhile, Sue had been attempting, without success, to obtain hot water from the maze of less than state-of-the-art plumbing sticking out of the wall in the general vicinity of the bath.

I went back down the corridor to sort out the hot water problem at reception and noticed a young man going into one of the rooms halfway down the hall. At least there were other guests, I thought, so the place must be all right. The girl I spoke to was very sympathetic about the hot water and said that it had probably only just been turned on and that it took some time to heat up. This is the land of "mañana" after all, I thought, so back to the room I went and we waited a while longer. Nothing happened, so Sue went back down to reception and I set off in search of the boiler room.

I hadn't ventured far into the boiler room when I noticed that my stockinged feet were wet and to my horror it was fuel oil, not water. I found the leak, tightened a pipe joint, opened all the widows, turned on the boiler, left my oily socks in a corner and returned barefoot to our room.

Sue came back and remarked that she had seen other young men down the hall. More guests we thought. At least the place was filling up and with more rooms occupied we would feel a little more secure in this huge motel.

Bathed and changed we set out across the road to the petrol station for our pre-dinner drink and to ask about suitable restaurants. Only in Spain did it seem to be the custom to pull in for petrol and have a quick brandy or two as part of the overall refuelling process. We also found similar facilities in most supermarkets. What a good idea for mum to do the shopping while dad had a cognac and coffee or a beer or two on the same premises. Sainsbury, Tesco and other supermarkets please take note! It all seemed so natural.

We enjoyed our drink, watching the passing motorists fill up themselves and their cars and the pump attendant/barman advised us of a reasonable restaurant back in town. Refreshed, we set off for our dinner. The girls were back sitting outside the hotel with the puppy and waved to us as we left.

The restaurant was in the centre of town, which eventually we reached having to negotiate through crowds, floats, bands, dancers and a procession. I thought that carnivals happened only in films and television travel programmes but this was real and we were there, tired, hungry and trying to navigate against the flow.

The Spanish take their evening meal a good deal later than the average Brit or American so we did not feel too bad arriving at the restaurant around nine thirty. The night obviously was still young for the locals. The bar was crowded. However, in the restaurant, which was in a back room, only one large table was occupied, among many empty ones. Around fifteen tall, fit-looking young men sat together, obviously on an outing of some sort.

We sat down, ordered drinks and looked at the menu. A very tall young black man unwound himself from his chair at the men's table, ambled across to us and said, in a deep southern US accent.

"Gee it's nice to see you folks, where are y'all from?"

He had obviously heard us talking and had assumed we were from downtown USA. We politely told him that were from the old country but that we had many ties with the US and lots of friends there. He was obviously disappointed that we were not American but told us that none of the friends he was with spoke much English and it was great to talk to someone who did. We assumed he was from the air base but he explained that he was the coach for a local professional basketball team and this was their end of season dinner.

They continued with their meal and we translated the menu, with some difficulty, and ordered ours. The noise level from the basket-ballers' table increased, more people came into the restaurant and a good time was being had by all. Our food and wine arrived and we settled down to do justice to both. As in most Spanish small-town restaurants, the food really was good, the wine excellent and the atmosphere extremely convivial.

Suddenly there was silence; something dramatic seemed about to happen. I glanced over to the big table and they were all sitting motionless, their desserts in front of them obviously waiting for a signal of some sort to begin their last course. I thought how polite it was for a large group of, by now, alcoholically inflamed young men to observe the niceties of etiquette whilst dining in public. Perhaps there was to be a speech or someone was about to say grace, even at this late stage in their celebrations.

A signal was given and two men on opposite sides at one end of the table picked up their plates, quickly swallowed their desserts, placed the plates upside down on their heads and then on the table in front of them. Immediately, the next two in line did the same and so did each diner, on down the entire length of the table. Much raucous cheering erupted on completion of this bizarre exercise.

Now, I've heard of schooner races, even taken part in a few in my time but they are normally conducted using pints of beer and in pubs or clubs, not with food in public restaurants! Whether it's an old Spanish or American custom to use desserts instead of beer I'll never know but it certainly was different!

The more sensible contestants had chosen crème caramel but a few had foolishly selected ice cream and at least one unfortunate diner had apple pie. Techniques varied from the oyster swallowing routine to the frantic shovelling method but the end result was much the same. Cheering, food everywhere, back-slapping and a few green faces. One contestant rather prematurely hurriedly left the table, never to be seen again.

We tried not to look too amused as several elderly Spanish diners obviously did not approve but it was rather funny and no damage was caused. The proprietor did not seem to mind either and as we left later through the bar, the survivors of the schooner race were still there enjoying themselves. If I'd been twenty years younger I might have joined them.

There's that old story about the three things that happen as you get older. The first is that you start to lose your memory. The second is that you … Darn it! What was the second thing?

But there is a fourth consequence of ageing, among the many more, that affects all of us. I well remember being able to go out most nights, sinking a good few ales, staying up late and then being able to get up early for work the morning after, feeling fresh and ready for anything. Not any more, so I didn't mind those younger men making the most of their youth - as long as they didn't bother anyone else too much whilst they had their fun.

Meanwhile, back at the motel, the bar and restaurant were still in full silence and the place seemed as empty as when we had left for our trip into town. However, the girls were still around and one or two different young men were in evidence. Hairdressing, we thought. What an enterprising sideline these girls had, in what would have otherwise been a dull old motel. That explained the comings and goings through the evening.

It was not until a little while later when we were in bed that it suddenly dawned on us that it wasn't scissors the girls were using to accommodate the young men but something far more basic and definitely more rewarding than hairdressing.

We were staying in a brothel!

We now understood why the girls spoke very good English, albeit it with American accents.

There was nothing we could do about it so we turned up the air conditioning, switched off the light and went to sleep.

In the morning the girls were both in reception and the little dog was amusing itself skidding across the ample marble floor. We declined breakfast, paid our bill and Sue asked casually what the puppy's name was?

"Eros," one of the girls said.

We should have known!

Chapter Ten

Deepest Sussex

Most of the houses we have looked after have been in the south of England, principally because our small but notable band of clients originated there and word of mouth has been our best and only publicity. Eventually, we could not keep up with demand and had to turn people down more often than we would have wished. We even had people re-arrange holiday dates so that we could fit in with their plans, or the other way round, to be more precise! In fact, we believe that some people began not to recommend us to their friends in order to avoid the possibility of us not being available for them in the future.

Notwithstanding, or forgetting, the beautiful landscapes in Kent, Berwickshire and Yorkshire, our own adopted county, we think that Sussex, particularly East Sussex, contains some of the finest houses and countryside we have experienced.

"And by-and-by they came to an enchanted place on the very top of the Forest called Galleon's Lap."

Words written some years ago by A A Milne in one of his books about Christopher Robin and Winnie the Pooh. Pooh Bridge is only about half a mile from my sister's place near Hartfield and many of our charges lived in the vicinity. Galleon's Lap is a delightful spot high up on Ashdown Forest, which looks north over a wide valley towards more of the forest rising away in the distance.

It **is** a wondrous place. In the early mornings the mist lingered in the valley below until the sun gracefully swept it away to reveal the gorse, heather and pine trees. The occasional splendid country house nestled on the opposite hillside. It was up here, one year, that we actually saw a cuckoo fly overhead. We'd often heard them before but had never set eyes on one.

As the late afternoon sun dipped to the west the evening shadows lengthened and stole across the valley. The colours softened and peace seemed to re-establish itself after the "hustle and bustle" of the bird and insect noises of the day.

Pooh Bridge attracts an astonishing number of visitors from all over Britain and around the world. I wonder how many are disappointed as it is really only a simple wooden bridge across a not too spectacular, common-or-garden country stream. Not a small stick was to be seen anywhere around the bridge. The surrounding trees also always looked suspiciously bare where, no doubt, over the years small children had sought desperately for their own Pooh sticks to throw into the water from the upstream side of the bridge. I've even seen Sue dash across to the downstream side to see if her sticks had floated successfully through to the other side.

Among the many tourists, we often saw visitors from Japan, some of whom had trekked on foot from Hartfield some three or four miles away and we wondered whether they thought their several thousand mile journey had been worth the time, expense and effort. More than once we encountered some who were completely lost and who would ask, "Prease can you tell us if this is the light load for Pooh Blidge?"

The magic of Christopher Robin and Winnie the Pooh still seems to capture the imagination of today's children just as it did all those years ago. Furthermore, with the likelihood of more films in the pipeline I can only see the number of tourists heading for Pooh land increasing – much to the consternation of some of the local residents.

A A Milne certainly knew a thing or two about choosing where to live and we can understand why so many other people decide to buy houses in this part of the world. We're glad that they did and that most of our "houses" were in that area.

One particular house we looked after nestled on a south-facing hillside looking towards the South Downs and the quiet village of Fletching. Dating back to the sixteenth century this timber framed old farmhouse with its crooked brick Tudor chimney, brick and plaster facing and stone footings, stood in colourful mature gardens with its original oast houses alongside. Inside, an impressive open old stone fireplace dominated the huge, timber-floored drawing room and another with a wood-burning stove graced the dining cum sitting room. Double French windows led from the drawing room, complete with low-beamed ceiling and wooden pillars, through a delightful, red terracotta tile floored conservatory on to a stone flagged terrace that ran round three sides of the house.

From the terrace, a large lawn with ample rose, flower and shrubbery beds sloped away to a small vegetable garden concealed behind a mature green and copper beech hedge. Further down the slope a small orchard sat beyond a tennis court and the valley receded into the distance to the downs on the horizon. Fletching church steeple rose in centre stage of this beautiful landscape, which might have been used by Constable as a source of inspiration for one of his masterpieces – if he ever came to Sussex.

The view varied continually depending on the time of day and changing weather conditions. In the early mornings we would see a hazy, surreal canvas, particularly when hedgerows and the steeple rose eerily out of the mist, which hugged the landscape like a translucent cotton-wool blanket. As the sun rose over the downs, Jack and Jill windmills stood out in the distance. In the bright sunlight of late morning the scenic panorama would present crisp contrasting greens and the sharp outlines of fields, hedgerows and trees stretching way into the distance. Then, late in the afternoon and early evening, the softening light would turn everything down a shade or two. Long shadows would provide depth and contrast to the landscape and the oranges and reds would begin to appear, both on the ground and in the sky.

On the second floor of the house every doorway invited one to "duck or grouse" and most rooms had exposed wall, as well as ceiling beams. On the landing a patch of the old wall had been left in its original condition showing the lath, plaster and straw of yesteryear's interior design. As the old beams were, presumably intentionally, bowed to hold a heavy load, all of the upstairs floors rose to the centre of the room and down again as they approached the windows.

Our only charge there was a delightful golden retriever called Tatti, short for Miss Tattinger, who we first met as a boisterous eight months old puppy. In her early days nothing was safe. Shoes, hats or anything else moveable had to be out of reach, and discipline, or the lack of it, was a real problem. She so much reminded me of my young Labrador, Jason, all those years before.

We were with Tatti one day out of sight of the house about halfway down the garden watching the huge white wind vanes atop the adjacent oast houses swing lazily in the breeze. Tatti heard a noise from the direction of the house. She ran at full speed up the garden when, without warning, the "home help" emerged from behind a hedge. Too late for Tatti to stop or change direction, and the unfortunate lady was completely up-ended. Both legs were swept from underneath her and she appeared to rise about four feet in the air ending up horizontally for what seemed an age before hitting the ground with a thud. Tatti, of course, thought this was all a great game but the poor lady was quite shaken, although thankfully she was not seriously hurt.

Fortunately, Tatti soon grew out of her "childish" ways and became a mature young lady and a credit to her owners' patience and training. She became a pleasure to look after and a joy on walks in the surrounding beautiful countryside. She was undoubtedly the best looking dog we ever looked after.

Tatti

Tatti's owners were really organised. Not that other owners weren't, I hasten to add, but at Tatti's house everything was in its place and labelled, even in the tool shed. Our notes were always comprehensive and envelopes were always left for disbursements to gardeners, cleaners etc. On first seeing these neatly stacked envelopes with instructions on the outside I was reminded of a "true" story which I heard during my former career as a "highly stressed executive".

On taking up a particularly difficult appointment I was handed three envelopes by my predecessor numbered one, two and, as you might gather, three.

My outgoing colleague said, "If you get into difficulties with the job and you can't see a way out, open the envelopes in order for each insurmountable problem you come across."

I lasted about six months before my first big problem occurred. Things weren't going well at all and I just could not see a solution, so I thought it was time to open the first envelope. Inside was a card, which said simply:

"Blame your predecessor."

Not my usual style, but I did and it worked. The pressure eased and things went fine for another year. The tide was going against me, the walls were closing in, my boss and I did not agree and at last I had to open the second envelope.

The card inside said:

"Tell them you are re-organising."

Brilliant, I thought. That should work. There's always chaos during a re-organisation and I'd been in the job long enough to be able to justify such a ploy. My excuse worked, I seemed to be swimming with the current again and there was peace in the office - for a while.

Another year passed and things started to go really badly, worse than on the two previous occasions. Head Office was on my back, my boss's boss wasn't speaking to me, or him, and I had completely lost direction. There was only one thing for it. I had to open the last envelope. The message on the card inside was simple:

"Prepare three envelopes."

No, it probably never happened, certainly not to me but I thought it was a good story!

****

One year we had some friends from California visit us during a trip in which they were "doing Europe." You know, if it's Tuesday its Paris, that type of thing. The only time they could come to see us was while we were in East Sussex. We therefore fixed them up with a bed and breakfast in Fletching and showed them around that beautiful part of the country in the three days they were to be in our neck of the woods.

As with many Americans, they were fascinated with our history. The cliché is so true that in the UK a hundred miles is a long way; in the USA a hundred years is a long time. You don't find many (any) houses or churches in the US, particularly in California, dating back to the fifteen hundreds. And 1066, forget it!

Our friends were fascinated to learn that in 1264 on the eve of the battle of Lewes, Simon de Montfort had camped with his army at Fletching. The village became known in medieval times for the manufacture of arrowheads, and there is a theory that the village owes its name to the French word fleche. Even if not, Fletching arrowheads were used by English archers during the Hundred Years War.

Chuck and Linda wanted to soak in all this history and brass rubbing was high on their list of wanna-dos. We had previously visited the church in Fletching and knew that it contained some superb brasses so we telephoned the vicar to enquire whether an appointment was necessary to "rub" in his church. He advised us of the best times to visit and what the fees were so off we set with our friends, armed with the necessary black paper, Sellotape and wax crayons to copy a little bit of our history to be destined for the walls of their Californian home.

Fletching church dates back to early Norman or late Saxon times and we had selected a late fourteenth century brass on the tomb of a knight and his lady of the Dalyngrugge family as a fitting memento for our friends.

We'd been rubbing for about an hour when in strolled a short, rotund man in T-shirt and shorts and asked us after a while how we were doing. We said fine, and that we had cleared our visit with the vicar. He said,

"I am the vicar."

(Where have I heard that before? Probably, in some smutty joke.) We complimented him on his fine church, handed over our fee, trying not to giggle, and all was well.

Chuck and Linda's visit would not have been complete without a visit to Lewes, Battle Castle and lunch and dinner at local pubs. We did all of that with them, although I missed out on most of the historical bits as we did not both like to be away from our houses or charges for longer than is necessary to shop, dog walk or eat out occasionally during our stays. We had dinner in a pub at Fletching and, exceptionally for Britain we were able to sit outside enjoying a sundowner before ,dinner with the sun actually in view while it went down over the garden, trees and fields of the South Downs beyond.

Our friends, as many foreign visitors must, asked us why the Downs are called Downs when in fact they are most definitely "Ups". Fortunately, we knew the answer. Apparently, the name comes from the Saxon word dun, which means an open, treeless, sometimes farmed hillside. As long ago as the fifth century the Saxons began colonising parts of Sussex, Surrey and Kent in Southern England. Similarly, the adverb "down" is thought to have come from the Saxon word dune or "from off the hill".

Lunch, one day, was a special treat for our visitors as the weather was also kind enough to allow us to eat outside a pub in the village of East Dean. It was a Sunday and, almost as if on cue, we were treated to local folk music and Morris dancing on the village green opposite the pub during our meal. Good beer, excellent food, a glorious English summer's day, local colour and music and good company.

Chuck and Linda were amazed that we allowed dogs in pubs but not children, although that has been relaxed a bit these days. It's certainly not that way in the US.

What a way to spend a Sunday lunchtime. Our American friends loved it, although I must admit I had to tell them that not all English musicians and dancers wore bells, ribbons, knee-length trousers, funny hats and carried hoops of flowers.

Chuck and Linda were also impressed by one or two other things rarely seen at home in the good old US of A. We took them to Beachy Head by way of Wilmington and they were fascinated by the well-endowed man of Wilmington etched on the hillside, which they photographed from all angles.

They were more surprised than impressed by the antics of some of the locals on the beach beneath the cliffs at Beachy Head. Chuck was surveying the scene on the bright, warm summer's afternoon that we were there when suddenly he said,

"Linda, there are people down there with no clothes on."

Sure enough, below us was a nudist beach or at least a beach with naked people on it! At that point Linda grabbed the binoculars, "just to check it out." Now, despite all the up-to-date, fashionable, state of the art life styles in the US, nudist beaches are definitely not on. Even in laid back, way-out California, there are not even any topless beaches, let alone any allowing the full Monty.

We just had to climb down the many wooden steps to the cobbled beach below where they insisted on having their picture taken with the stark white Seven Sisters in the distance, probably together with at least half a dozen stark naked brothers and sisters in the foreground. We never did see the photographs!

On a tamer note, our friends could not believe the width of the country lanes around Fletching. Two-way traffic on lanes so narrow that the bracken brushed both sides of our car was commonplace in this part of the world. They could not believe it but to us, having lived in Devon, it seemed perfectly acceptable.

Before they arrived in England we had corresponded by e-mail (can't live without it) and they had said several times that they would hire a car from Gatwick and drive it around the south east of England. We had insisted that it would be just as easy for us to pick them up and run them around during their short stay. After their arrival it took only a few miles for Chuck to express his deep gratitude for our persistence as he admitted he could not have driven a non-automatic, right-hand drive car on our narrow town and country roads.

****

This part of the East Sussex countryside is perfect for hot air ballooning. Sheffield Park near Fletching provides the perfect lift-off site and on many a fine summer's evening balloons would take off and drift lazily overhead on their way to wherever hot air balloons go. Some would hang motionless overhead and only the occasional blast of burning propane would advertise their presence in the otherwise peaceful landscape. We had been warned that Tatti did not like hot air balloons but were not really prepared for her reaction to the first one that appeared during one of our stays.

We were sitting peacefully in the garden late one afternoon. We seemed to do a lot of that on our visits. However, I do hasten to repeat that we did have the occasional bursts of energy and managed quite a bit of voluntary gardening and compulsory dog walking. Three of "our" houses also boasted tennis courts and we have been known to work up a lather in that way, particularly around Wimbledon time when the whole nation is reminded that tennis is not a bad way of getting exercise. In our younger days we preferred squash as the ball was always to hand somewhere close by. Whereas when playing tennis, the ball tends to go over the wire occasionally or is always in the farthest corner of the court. Squash also always seemed to be the quickest way to get lots of exercise in the shortest time.

Anyway, there we were at peace with the world when suddenly Tatti exploded in a burst of frenzied barking. She ran around the garden staring up at the sky and disappeared round the side of the house to emerge a few seconds later to repeat the exercise. We looked up and way in the distance, looking like little dots of colour against the sky, we could see a couple of balloons heading our way. Too far away to be heard by us but Tatti had clearly seen or heard them and was either protecting her territory or was scared stiff, or both. As the multi-coloured balloons approached Tatti gave in and retreated into the house where she hid amongst the gate legs under a stout oak dining table. She would emerge every now and then to check whether the coast was clear but would not join us again until the sky was its normal uncluttered self again.

We can only guess that at some time in her life a low flying balloon's burner being ignited immediately overhead may have surprised Tatti. There seemed to be no other explanation for her behaviour as low flying helicopters and aircraft left her unmoved.

My sister had taken a trip in a hot air balloon some time previously and she recounted that one of the lasting memories of that trip was the number of dogs that barked as the balloon passed overhead. Apart from short noisy periods whilst the gas jet burned to heat up the air inside the balloon most of her trip was in complete silence. No wind noise either as, in theory, the balloon travels at the same speed as the wind.

Another comment she made which might be of interest to prospective hot air balloonists was that she wished that she and her husband had worn a hat of some kind as protection from the heat of the burner!

Some of the balloons really did fly low overhead. One day we were watching an extremely low flying balloon when a head appeared over the rim of the basket and the pilot, obviously wishing to land, shouted down to us asking if we knew of any fields round about without cattle, sheep or crops.

We said, "In this area? Not a chance, good luck!" He piled on the propane and we never saw him again.

One of the drawbacks of owning a Labrador or golden retriever is that at certain times of the year house, car, clothes and other areas tend to suffer from an abundance of dog hair. Golden retrievers are probably the worst and Tatti was no exception. Despite regular brushing she seemed to have an everlasting coat and although she was not allowed in all parts of the house, most rooms seemed to get covered in dog hairs when she was moulting. It was times like this that we were able to evaluate different vacuum cleaners and firmly believe that all vacuum cleaner manufacturers' research and development organisations should have golden retrievers as permanent members of their staff.

Tatti, like all other dogs, was always brushed outside in the garden and although large clumps of hair ended up in the rubbish bin, inevitably there would always be a thin sheen of blonde hair left on the lawn after a grooming session.

Talking of blonde hair, we were in a local pub one evening when we overheard someone say that there's no such thing as a smart blonde. There was a short silence and then a voice piped up from the other end of the bar.

"Oh yes there is. I know one; my golden retriever."

Back to the script! The day after one such brushing we noticed a small finch strutting about the lawn sporting what looked like a blonde moustache. It had been collecting Tatti's off-cast hair, strand by strand, in its beak and looked like a cross between Jimmy Edwards and Raymond Glendenning. (They were even before my time.) Unaware of our presence, the tiny bird filled its beak to the brim and took off, presumably to line its nest with its new-found carpet. Oh for a long-range telephoto lens on hand. We could have won the photo of the year competition hands down.

One of the drawbacks with large female dogs, particularly where pristine lawns are concerned, is the regular appearance of brown circles on the grass. Short of fencing lawns off, or one hundred per cent surveillance it was very difficult, if not impossible, to keep Tatti from relieving herself with the resulting brown, dead grass circles appearing at the spot a day or two later.

Fascinating subject! However, all female dog owners, or should I be more specific and say owners of female dogs, will know of the problem. In rainy weather the situation was not so bad but given the long dry spells of summer (hopefully) it could be a real pain to try to alleviate the problem. I've even been known to dash out with the watering can on many occasions in an attempt to dilute the deposit.

You might have noticed that around the edge of the circle of dead grass there is usually a ring of grass which appears lush and in better condition than the rest of the lawn. If only we could catch and dilute the product before it hits the grass we could really solve the problem, and probably make a ton of money in the process.

One idea Tatti's owner came up with, although it didn't seem to work while we were there, was to add tomato juice to her food. We found that the only sure-fire cure was to scrape away the dead grass after a few days, put down some fresh potting soil and re-seed the area. Three weeks later the offending patch would be as good as new.

Having mentioned that Tatti had grown into a well-mannered young lady, she was almost uncontrollable where sheep, rabbits, cats and other pursuable animals were concerned. We didn't get many rabbits in the vegetable patch as a result but walks had to be carefully watched where other animals were likely to be present. Fortunately, the countryside round about presented ample opportunity for keeping away from farm animals yet contained miles of tracks in unspoiled woodland in which to roam.

Often Tatti would disappear in pursuit of rabbit or deer but would eventually return at a blast from her whistle. She never caught anything but we often saw deer that might have otherwise remained invisible to us bounding away from her through the undergrowth with graceful ease. The deer were even more beautiful in full flight than when standing still and we saw many more during our stays with Tatti.

Sometimes, we'd see a single glorious buck with antlers proud. At other times we would come across whole families standing motionless under the trees, their camouflage almost making them "disappear" in the dappled sunlight on the surrounding leaves and branches. Only when they moved could their shapes be seen clearly. We wondered how many more deer we had passed on our many walks without seeing them, hidden under their canopy of invisibility.

We saw many more deer during our spells at various other houses in East Sussex. Perhaps the most memorable was the pair that used to appear at the front of one house in the middle of the night. Their arrival always activated the security lights. They were oblivious to the bright light and just carried on grazing on the grass at the edge of the drive, no more that twenty feet from our bedroom window. Animals are always best observed in their natural habitat when unaware that they are being watched. These were no exception. They were graceful, elegant and completely at ease. We didn't mind being awakened by them and we took great pleasure in their presence.

A couple of nights later a mature male fox provided us with the same chance to watch him unawares. He was in prime condition, his red and brown coat in stark contrast against the heavy white frost. Although foxes are not farmers' best friends, they are beautiful animals and it is not often one gets a chance to see more than their rear ends as they take flight in the presence of danger.

Just a few miles northeast from Tatti's house lies the quiet, picturesque village of Horsted Keynes (pronounced Canes) in West Sussex. We had the good fortune to look after a couple of golden retrievers in a house not far from the church. That gave us the chance to explore the village and the surrounding countryside during one of the hottest weeks for several years. Not far from the village, several lakes nestled in a valley, providing excellent interesting dog walks.

Old churches had become a must for our attentions in each new place we visited. More for the history and atmosphere than for spiritual sustenance and there was always a sense of quiet, peace and tranquillity in these churches and churchyards which is difficult to find nowadays in our high-speed society. Castles and ruins provide the same sort of calming effect and if you ever want to slow yourself down, take a breather or just give yourself time to think, try making an occasional visit to one of these beautiful old buildings. You might be surprised at the effect it can have.

Unusually, the church at Horsted Keynes is at a lower level than most of the remainder of the village and it is approached down a delightful lane complete with cottages and a huge graceful old country-house rectory standing proud in its own substantial grounds. The churchyard itself is surrounded by a circular ditch, which suggests that the site dates back to pre Christian times. Parts of the church do date back to the Norman period but it is mostly thirteenth century and constructed of local stone with a pointed spire on the tower. In the north wall of the chancel lies a tiny cross-legged figure only twenty seven inches long, thought by some to be the remains of Richard de Keynes, the last of the family which gave its name to the village. However, others believe it may be a heart shrine, containing all that was returned of a Knight in Armour who never came back from the Holy Land during the crusades.

Many other famous people were buried here in this quiet corner of rural England. The remains of some of the Wyatts, descendants of Sir Thomas, beheaded by Queen Mary, lie here together with those of Robert Leighton, Archbishop of Glasgow, who died in 1684. Their long-time resting place is shared by relative newcomers; Sir Harold and Lady Macmillan who lie in their family plot in the churchyard looked over by a huge mature yew tree.

Two good pubs, a small selection of village shops and a post office complete the village picture and Horsted Keynes ranks highly on our list of desirable places to live if, or when, we ever settle down.

Chapter Eleven

The Sunshine State

During our three-year stay in the United States some years previously, we had acquired a taste for the climate and relaxed way of life in southwest Florida. In more recent years we feel very fortunate, therefore, to have been able to spend a good portion of our winters there, in Naples on the west coast, just about as far away from the glitz and commercialisation of Miami as one can get before falling into the Gulf of Mexico. Naples is a small town with a delightful, relatively old-world "down town" area with strict planning or "zoning" codes to preserve its particular charm and almost continental atmosphere. Away from the town centre, however, and unfortunately, money hungry property developers pursue their relentless quest for profit at the expense of the wetlands and wildlife.

Golf course communities and shopping malls are springing up, as if overnight, as more and more snowbirds from the northern United States and Canada realise that Florida is the place to be to avoid their bitter winters back home. Fortunately, there is still plenty of space and it will be a long while before this part of the world becomes like too many others, over-populated and devoid of wildlife.

****

It was in Naples, late one afternoon that Sue and I were watching the sun begin its gradual descent across the lake and beyond the grass and pine trees in the distance. We were in for another glorious southwest Florida sunset. A kingfisher launched itself, with wings swept back like a fighter aircraft and plunged into the lake from a branch not twenty feet from us to seek its supper. The ibis and blue heron were out there too, fishing more sedately along with the anhinga and occasional cormorant.

In the pine trees opposite, we could hear, but not yet see, a pair of great horned owls calling to each other as they did often at this time of the day. On many an evening they were in full view and Sue and I watched them with our binoculars. They were magnificent creatures almost two feet tall with their prominent ear feathers making them look like two large cats perched high in the pine trees.

An alligator, only its snout above the water, glided effortlessly right in front of us, probably not in search of his supper as a Muscovy duck and her young brood swam contentedly not too far away, near the wooden bridge in the centre of our view.

As the sun sank lower and lower in the western sky it expanded, slowly turned to red and the shadows lengthened. The owls moved closer to us, calling to each other from adjacent trees presumably preparing themselves for their nightly hunting. Soon they would be silent. They would then concentrate, from on high, on their deadly quest for the other creatures of the night upon which they feed. The undergrowth beneath the trees would afford little protection to their prey.

In the morning we saw an osprey high overhead as he too searched the lake for easy prey. At that time of year, with the waters high, there was plenty for him, the other birds and the kingfisher. We'd seen ospreys dive from forty or fifty feet, talons outstretched, hit the water with an almighty splash and take off again with a hapless fish clutched in those deadly claws.

They were smart enough to carry their prey "fore and aft" to reduce drag until they found a secure perch upon which to consume their catch. The turkey vultures could then often be seen waiting for crumbs from the osprey's table upon which to scavenge, as they do not hunt themselves. Later that day we caught a glimpse of a bald eagle as he soared high above, confident that he had no predators and that he could rule the skies with confidence.

Where were we? No, we were not in some exotic nature reserve or wildlife park. All this from our own screened porch, or lanai as they are called in that part of the country. You might therefore understand why Sue and I crossed the Atlantic each winter, whenever we could. Not only to escape the fog, cold and damp of a good portion of the British winter but to experience the sights and sounds of nature that we could not enjoy, in comfort, in good old Yorkshire at that time of year.

Mentioning Yorkshire brings me around to Liz, our first ward in the United States. We had not expanded our house sitting into a transatlantic operation but inevitably we talked to our neighbours and friends about our experiences and it was not long before we were asked to look after one of their dogs.

Liz, a tiny Yorkshire terrier, unlike our British charges, came to stay with us instead of us living in its house whilst her owners were away. Liz's owners were a feisty, older couple who, in their late 70's still travelled the world. They spent some of the winter in the warmth of Florida but often braved the harsh New England climate in January and February to go skiing. It must have been that they have continued skiing through middle age that enabled them still to participate in a sport that fells many younger mortals. They also spent a good deal of time on the slopes in Italy. So much so, that they had their other sets of skis and equipment stored over there.

On this occasion, when Liz came to stay with us, her owners were on their way to Branson, Missouri. For those not au fait with American music, this is the Country and Western concert capital of the world! There are constant shows all day and on a six-day trip it is not unheard of to take in ten different shows during one visit. The Americans have such a slick way of operating their show business ventures, as can be seen from the Disney theme parks. Within this one small backwoods town they have created a Country and Western, and other smoother music, tourist heaven. There is everything from music shows to superb tourist "accommodations" with every other tourist trap in between. Coach trips are run from all over the States and this old quiet Ozark town is now a twenty-four hour music city! Not usually the place for seventy-plus year olds, one would think, but as in all tourist places there are the inevitable up-market hotels and restaurants to satisfy all tastes.

We had been to Branson many years previously, on an autumn trip to the Tantara Resort to play golf. Back in the early 80's it was a beautiful place along the shores of the Lake of the Ozarks. We spent an idyllic weekend there, playing golf and walking in the glorious fall coloured woods. These pastimes were followed by drinks and extremely well cooked meals served by a blazing log fire. It was there, in our chalet on the lakeshore that we were amused by a carved sign over the dining area: Bon Appetite – Y'all.

Our abiding memories of the resort are of not being able to walk the golf course, as in places there were not only steep hills but also half- mile treks through the woods from the green to the next tee. Electric carts were the order of the day therefore, as they are on most American golf courses, and the drinks cart complete with optics came round on a regular basis. Oh for that on a cold, wet, British golf course! I suppose it is still all there but now within a stone's throw of a Country and Western theme park.

So Liz came to stay while her owners went line dancing! Liz settled in, but not completely. She would not eat her food unless she was hand fed. Her owners had made up fourteen packs of "Lizzie food" (tiny portions of human food really, chicken, pasta and the like) and she had one twice a day. The amounts were so small, even for a tiny dog, that hand feeding was not too much of a problem. Walking the dog, albeit with compulsory "pooper-scoopers", was also only a small burden! The only untoward thing about her was that she would not tolerate invasion of her territory.

Now remember, even though this dog was a full seven inches tall at the shoulder she was still a terrier deep down and what do terriers do? They dig and tear. Well, Liz took exception to our gardeners. We had a full-length window alongside the front door, covered by a Venetian blind. We left Liz in and went to play golf, the gardeners came and Liz could hear them but needed to "see" them off!

We arrived back home to find the Venetian blind with its bottom six slats mangled and totally unidentifiable! Never let it be said that small dogs are not good guard dogs. Anything, of any size, can be frightening with sharp pointed teeth, or so the gardeners told us later!

Other than that small incident, for which her owners well recompensed us, Liz was a joy to have around and even graduated to being allowed to sleep on our bed. Normally unheard of in our household! Mind you, this was partly for our comfort as she would bark outside our bedroom door to be let in and then try and jump on to the bed once inside. There really was no alternative to her sharing our bed. Thankfully, she did not insist on getting under the covers!

At the end of her stay, Liz walked happily back to her owners, there was a joyful reunion and we said good-bye to our first overseas client.

I mentioned alligators earlier and yes, there were some to be seen cruising the lakes around where we lived during our stays. They presented no real danger as long as they were treated with the respect they deserved and anyway, once they reached a certain length, around four feet I believe, they were caught and released further east into the Everglades. However, all the lakes, rivers and canals throughout the area were linked by culverts and all the rainwater falling in the Everglades (and there was lots of it) passed by us on its way to the Gulf. There was therefore always ample opportunity for the alligators to find their way back.

One evening, one of our neighbours was sitting with his wife on their lanai enjoying their pot roast dinner by candlelight when they were startled by a grunt-like noise coming from the direction of the lake. They were alarmed. Especially when the noise came closer to them and grew louder. Fearing it was an alligator attracted by the aroma coming from their food, they picked up everything, retreated indoors and continued their dinner in safety. When they recounted their ordeal to me the next day I asked them to reproduce the sound they had heard. It was all I could do to avoid cracking up and bursting out with laughter when they gave a perfect imitation of a bullfrog. I'm not sure, however, whether they still eat outdoors!

Let us not take the alligator lightly though. They can move with alarming speed both in and out of the water and will attack if cornered or provoked.

We had some good friends, Ron and Gail from Pennsylvania, visiting us in Florida one winter and we were doing the tourist bit showing them the sights. Earlier that morning we had read in the local paper the sad story of a local elderly lady, living in a more remote part of the county, who had lost part of her arm to an alligator. The article told how one year previously she had been drawing water from a creek at the bottom of her property and had not noticed an alligator resting under the low bridge upon which she was standing. The beast had bitten off her arm just below the elbow. Apparently, they caught the alligator and retrieved her wedding ring but I guess that was small compensation for the loss of her limb.

Anyway, we had set off for the Everglades to show our guests real alligator territory and on our way east and well off the beaten track we saw a large homemade sign advertising BEER WORMS. As you might understand we were curious about this and wondered whether it was a local delicacy of which we had not heard. They do eat some strange things in the lesser-known parts of the United States, at least compared to our European tastes. Of course, they say the same about us, particularly with regard to the French. It took us a while to realise that the sign was aimed at two of the most popular local red-neck pastimes, beer drinking and fishing and that the two were not directly connected to human consumption.

Just a little way down what was by now a single-track country road we spotted an old lady hanging out washing in an overgrown front yard (garden) next to a dilapidated trailer (mobile home) and, yes, you've guessed it, she only had one arm! We were too polite to stop and ask whether she was the unfortunate lady we had just read about earlier that morning but we were pretty sure she was, unless arm biting was more prevalent than we were aware.

We progressed with our journey, off-road by now, on to a narrow dirt track leading right through the swamp. Travelling as slowly and as quietly as possible we looked out into the swamp on both sides and were rewarded by the sight of several small alligators posing obligingly in the sun on rocks and fallen trees, of which there were many. We also saw many swamp birds and turtles along the way.

Suddenly we spotted a huge 'gator. It must have been at least twelve feet long and was only about thirty feet into the swamp, clearly visible even without our binoculars. We backed up a little and got out of our mini-van to get a better look and take the inevitable photographs as evidence of our sighting. Ron, our visitor was very reluctant to leave the safety of the van but eventually was persuaded to do so. We'd only been clicking away for a minute or two when suddenly the beast swished its tail and slid quickly into the clear black water.

You've never seen four people move so fast! Within seconds we were all aboard the van with the doors shut tight. Needless to say, we never saw the alligator again.

Presumably it had just become bored with our presence and as we presented no threat had disappeared further into its domain.

We stopped to buy the compulsory postcards at a shop on the borders of the swamp on our journey back to "civilisation" and the store assistant did not believe our story, saying that alligators of that size do not venture near roads. We could not convince him that we had been off-road and were telling the truth but we did not bother to go back later to show him the pictures as proof of our experience.

Our next encounter with animals, worthy of note in Florida, excepting of course all of our neighbours' dogs, was through a chance meeting on the beach watching another beautiful sunset.

I suppose it happens in other parts of the world but it never ceased to amuse us that the sunset watchers, and there were many each evening, would applaud just after the sun dipped below the horizon. I have to say though (and I hate that expression) that the Naples sunsets are among the most beautiful I have seen in the world and I include Africa, the Mediterranean, the Caribbean, New Zealand and Australia in that comparison.

Best in the height of summer, with higher humidity and with the right combination of cloud formations, it was always a real joy to watch the golden globe disappear sedately into the sea. The colours in the sky would then slowly change from yellow, to orange, to gold and then red before the receding daylight wiped the canvas clean until dawn.

Back to the dogs. Next to us on the beach one evening were two dogs attached to a colourful character, bearing a striking resemblance to Beethoven, sporting shoulder length hair and dressed with an artistic flair. Lest I attract the local sheriff's attention to a potential minor misdemeanour, as dogs were not allowed on the beach, I should say we were all just off the sand seated on a bench thoughtfully provided for folks like us to applaud the daily late afternoon show.

The dogs came to talk to us, or more correctly it was probably Sue who went to talk to them. We soon struck up a conversation with Byron, their owner who turned out to be a composer and musician of some standing in his homeland, Canada, and who lived part of the year in Naples. The dogs were called Sushi, a sort of Tibetan terrier/ bearded collie mix and Chaucer, a Maltese terrier. Both dogs were very well behaved and super friendly and we very much enjoyed our discussion. We exchanged cards, said our farewells and went on our way.

Some weeks later we were surprised to receive a phone call from Byron asking us to come over to his place for a drink and then to walk with him and the dogs down to the beach again to watch the sunset. We were again very much impressed with the dogs and found Byron an immensely interesting character. We'd seen many intelligent well-trained dogs on our travels but Sushi really took the biscuit, literally.

When Byron sneezed, Sushi would rush off and come back with the box of tissues. He would fetch his lead on command and, when asked, barked his current age, how old he was last year and how old he would be next year. On questioning, however, Byron did confess later that for this particular trick Sushi had been three years old for the past few years! Artistic license, I guess. Nevertheless, we still thought it remarkable that the dog could remember the exact number of times to bark on hearing specific sentences.

In addition, Sushi had played the piano and had sung in one of the musical shows Byron had written and recorded in Canada. We have a copy of the tape to prove it! Both dogs sat together on Byron's knee and Sushi was an unashamed poser before the camera.

Chaucer, Byron and Sushi

Unfortunately, we never had the chance to look after these charming dogs, either in Florida or Canada, but maybe that pleasure will materialise sometime in the future.

Some years later, after we had cut our ties with Florida, having decided that there were other places in the world in which we should spend some time away from the UK in the bleak mid winter, we received an e-mail from Byron.

Apparently, some good friends of his from Toronto were retiring to Scotland and might want us to look after their pets. We didn't get in touch with them, as we really didn't want to expand our horizons, at that point, especially further north, but a little later we were contacted again by Byron. Some friends of his, Sue and Bob, were visiting the UK scouting for property and wanted us to meet them. They were going to be in Richmond for a couple of days during a week's visit to the old country, and would we like to meet them for dinner one evening?

We thought that Richmond, Surrey, was a long way to travel from Harrogate just for dinner and were just about to decline the invitation when he explained it was Richmond, Yorkshire. We were then delighted to drive up to one of our favourite parts of the UK and swiftly recommended a great gastro pub we knew, the Black Bull at Moulton. It is a well-known and long-standing interesting venue, part of the eating area is an old Pullman railway carriage and the other various nooks and crannies all have their own theme.

The food is varied and interesting. So, off we went and spent a very relaxed and enjoyable evening, as though we had known them for years. Of course, it helped that we shared a common acquaintance in Byron and a very apparent love of animals. At that time they had three dogs and seven cats and all were to be shipped across the Atlantic to take up a new life in Scotland!

We promised to keep in touch and soon the two Sues were e-mailing and swapping tales and news like old friends. They invited us up to see them when they moved over from Canada, and we looked forward to it. Eventually they moved lock, stock and barrel, to Dumfries from Toronto. Literally the stock, as the dogs and cats were crated and left Toronto on the same plane as their owners on the way to a new life. Byron told us it was a little like moving a zoo. Some of the pets showed no reaction, others were very vocal. Thankfully, all arrived safely, with the assistance of pet passports, a wonderful, forward- thinking way to allow animals to travel between countries.

We didn't have the chance to visit them when they first settled in but the opportunity arose some eighteen months later. We were travelling up to the north of Scotland for a week and arranged to see them on the way. Sue and Bob kindly invited us to have dinner with them and to stay the night and we readily accepted. We arrived in the glorious hill country of Dumfries and Galloway to find their fantastic house, packed with an eclectic collection of mementos of their varied and well-travelled life and, of course, full of animals; two gorgeous bearded collies, a

Norfolk terrier and, by now, six Persian cats of various colours.

We had a superb meal and a wonderful evening during which we watched the sun set across a valley and over the hills with the sky turning from blue to pink to gold and eventually cobalt blue. Afterwards we thought we would never have believed that we could have met someone, now a good friend, watching the sun set on a beach in south west Florida, through talking to his dogs, and as a result of which, some years later, we would end up sitting in south west Scotland watching the same sun set over a completely different, but equally as spectacular, view with two new friends.

But that's dogs for you!

Chapter Twelve

An Ecclesiastical Diversion

A couple we knew in the UK had mutual friends of ours visiting them from the USA one year. David and Ruth had decided to do something special for Ron and Gail as it was Ron's sixtieth birthday and Gail had brought her ageing parents along to tour England with them. As it was to be a surprise for Ron and party, all David had told them was that they would be going out to dinner, so they dressed accordingly. We were invited to join the party and were looking forward to a great evening.

David had a long haired collie dog who couldn't be left alone for long so they dropped the dog off at his parents' house on the way out that evening, a Saturday in late summer. We eventually pulled up outside a cathedral and we, and our American friends, were more than a little surprised at what appeared to be our evening's destination. We all trooped out of the two cars required to get us there and were ushered in to take our seats in the knave of the cathedral. The Dean then proceeded to celebrate Evensong! Ron half expected the proceedings to be interrupted by a stripper-gram or some such other entertainment at any time. After all, this was his sixtieth birthday and he had been promised something special!

However, the service proceeded to its conclusion; prayers were said for all kinds of people but no mention of Ron or the rest of the overseas visitors. After it was over we were all invited to remain behind as the Dean wished to show us over the cathedral. It suddenly dawned on me that this was part of the plan as David was a good friend of the Dean and, as a well-known businessman in the area, probably a substantial contributor to cathedral funds.

Now the ladies in the party were not dressed to sit through a church service and then tour a chilly, ancient building. Gail's feet were killing her in a tight fitting new pair of shoes and both she and her mother were shivering with cold. However, it's not often that American tourists get the chance to be shown round a cathedral by the Dean, no less, so they gritted their teeth and followed the rest of us to begin our tour. The Dean knew his stuff and took great pains to show us in his most theatrical style, every tomb, architectural feature and historical facet of the place. And, of course, there were many.

He laid great emphasis on the beauty of the crypt but as they emerged at the top of the stone staircase Gail remarked, "Gee that's some basement, but I thought we might at least see a few bones down there." In fact, it was pretty uninteresting, whitewashed walls and not much to see at all.

The Dean stopped and looked at her with that pained, knowing expression that many British people tend to reserve for use in recognition of the average American's naivety regarding things of great historical significance. He muttered something under his breath along the lines of; "My 1,200 year old crypt has been relegated to the status of a basement," and, with a shrug of his shoulders, walked on trying to ignore the comment.

Now, of course, there is no way I can tell you which cathedral it was or even in which county we were, to protect the innocent. More likely to avoid a law suit!

The tour at last over, we were then startled to learn that we were all to have dinner in the Dean's house in the cathedral grounds. David had organised a local first class hotel to provide the catering and drinks and the Dean had kindly agreed to provide the venue for our dinner. Unfortunately, our tour had overrun by at least half an hour, not least because of the Dean's enthusiasm for his subject and his descriptive eloquence.

The Dean's wife, Helen, had therefore been waiting patiently for us accompanied by their daughter and, by now, a nearly empty bottle of sherry. Helen was an attractive, elegant lady of generous proportions and her daughter, Muriel, was very prim and proper with hair tied tightly on the top of her head and school ma'am spectacles.

We sat down to eat and it was immediately obvious that Helen and Muriel were way past caring about our tardiness and were now enjoying white and red wine at unusual speed and in copious quantities, helped on by Gail's father who seemed keen to keep their glasses full.

The first course arrived, steaming hot and we looked forward to warming ourselves from the inside out with the delicious smelling soup placed in front of us together with hot crusty rolls. Alas, it was not to be. Before we could even lift a spoon or butter the scrumptious fresh baked bread we were assailed by the raucous shouts of a Town Crier. He appeared as if from nowhere and frightened the hell out of Gail's mother with his "Oyez, Oyez, Oyez," routine at full volume.

Fortunately, he did not have a bell with him as they often do when performing in the town square. For several minutes, which felt more like hours, he regaled us with the importance of the relationship with our American cousins, how honoured the city was to receive such distinguished visitors and generally cemented the Anglo/American relationships for at least the next twenty years.

Meanwhile, we were at a loss as to whether to start our meal or to sit tight and listen to the speech unfolding at a really unnecessary volume around the room. As one always should, we took our cue from our host and it was with some relief that eventually we saw the Dean pick up his spoon as the Crier's speech drew to a close. We set to and enjoyed our first course, albeit by now a little less than piping hot.

At one point during dinner the family cat jumped up on the table and laconically strolled between plates and dishes before deciding that she'd seen enough and returned to her rightful place before the fire. Mother and daughter thought that this was hilarious, the Dean seemed mildly annoyed and our American visitors were astounded.

Just before dessert was served, Helen returned to the table after, presumably, answering the call of nature and, on re-seating herself, misjudged the spot at which she thought the edge of her chair should be. Trying to look as dignified as possible under the circumstances and, by now also under the table, she managed to hook one foot and a hand on the edge of the table on her way floor-ward while the rest of her ample proportions were in disarray and on considerably embarrassing display to the rest of the company.

If you have ever been in similar circumstances you'll know how difficult it is to retain one's composure. However, she managed it, and, with great difficulty none of us uttered even a giggle and all offered concern about our hostess's welfare. The Dean, as you might expect, was not best pleased at his wife's deportment, or lack of it, and serious looks were exchanged from one end of the table to the other once the hapless woman had regained her composure and her seat at the second attempt.

As the meal progressed both mother and daughter became more and more "relaxed" as the wine kept flowing. By now Muriel had shucked off her hair band and had shaken her hair out to its full shoulder length and taken off her glasses. She looked a completely different person. Now, she was an extremely glamorous young lady and nothing like the typical vicar's, or in this case, Dean's daughter.

The meal over, Helen rose unsteadily to her feet approached her husband and muttered something inaudible to the rest of us. He motioned for her to bend closer and whispered something, equally inaudible, into her ear. At that she rose to her full height, drew back her arm, gave the Dean a severe crack around the ear with the palm of her hand and stormed out of the room without another word to anyone.

There is absolutely nothing else to do in those sort of circumstances, especially in the company of strangers, than to act as though absolutely nothing out of the ordinary had happened and that's exactly what we all did – the Dean included.

We never saw her again!

At long last the meal ended and we retired from the dining room for brandy, liqueurs and cigars into the library, by now, minus the lovely Muriel who had not returned from a presumed trip to the loo.

You must have been in a situation with a group of people where no-one wants to be the first to say anything, there's an embarrassing silence and the longer it goes on the worse it gets. Well, this was one of those – big time! There was at least half an hour to go before our pre-arranged limousine was to arrive and you could have cut the atmosphere with a knife.

At last, with an embarrassed "harrumph" and a cough or two the Dean broke the silence by asking somewhat apologetically whether we would like to look around the Deanery. Anything would have been better than the stony silence so we said yes, thank you, and trooped off after him on another tour. Fortunately this one was a tad more comfortable and very much more interesting than our chilly walk around the cathedral earlier in the evening. Apart from the design and architecture of the building itself, it contained a great deal of art and silver which made the tour very acceptable and gave the Dean the opportunity to regain his confidence and to elaborate on the many interesting aspects of his home.

Midnight arrived along with our limousine, which turned out to be a small mini-van, to take all eight of us to our respective destinations having consumed well over the legal, maybe even healthy, limits of various alcoholic liquids during the course of the evening. After thanking the Dean profusely for his hospitality, saying our goodbyes and tendering our good wishes to his family we crammed aboard and set off.

A while later David instructed the driver to stop at his mother's place and the driver asked who was getting out there.

"No-one," David said. "My dog is getting in."

The driver definitely didn't approve of that but there wasn't much he could do! Of course, as it was way past midnight David's parents were in bed and the house was in darkness so it took ages before they were awakened and the dog was persuaded to leave and climb aboard the van.

The rest of the journey was uneventful but we, and I'm sure our American friends, will never forget that truly memorable evening in the company of the Dean and his family.

It must have been more than an isolated performance from the Dean as I was not surprised to hear a few years later that he had "resigned" from his appointment under pressure from "above". Something to do with "conduct unbecoming etc, etc".

Chapter Thirteen

Things That Go Bump In The Night

The silence of the countryside at night brought its own problems to me, at least. As an extremely light sleeper, I had to put up with the occasional screech of an owl, the bark of a fox, restless cattle or sheep and the inevitable dawn chorus. As an early riser, I did not mind the dawn chorus, except, perhaps, at four in the morning during mid-summer. However, unfamiliar noises in the middle of the night were never to my liking. You might now more appreciate my comments a little earlier about noisy clocks.

Perhaps the worst animal offender in my disrupted sleep pattern was a dear little Border terrier called Fergie. He lived with his companion Otis, a young black male Labrador, in a magnificent old Manor House and we had looked after them both on different occasions over a couple of years.

Now Fergie was sixteen years old and had lost, or was in the process of losing, several of his faculties. Sight, and hearing were two of the more benign but bladder and bowel control came a close third and fourth and were not nearly so easy to deal with. However, if you've had dogs of your own you'll know that these things happen and there's nothing for it but to accept it as part of life. Cleaning up was an accepted part of the morning routine but, to be fair, it didn't happen that often and Fergie was a grand (but little) old "man" who had given his owners a great deal of love, affection, companionship and joy that long-term dog-ownership provides.

Fergie didn't sleep well though, and so neither did anyone else in the house. Like most terriers he had a loud, high-pitched bark that penetrated even to the third floor bedroom we occupied when in residence at the Manor. Once Fergie was awake he just had to let everyone know and would bark until he had human company. It seemed Otis's presence was not enough for him and Otis would often join in with the barking, if Fergie was ignored for any length of time.

Sadly, and I do very much mean that, Fergie's condition worsened and he had to be put to sleep between two of our visits only a couple of weeks apart. The house never seemed the same again. His owners were, understandably, considerably upset by his passing and I suspect that we would all have preferred the sleepless nights if little Fergie could have survived a while longer.

Otis, too, missed him terribly and went off his food for weeks. Although we do suspect he was glad to have a little peace as Fergie did use to bother him all day long.

On our first visit to the house after Fergie's departure the vet called to say that his ashes were available for collection. We didn't feel that we should undertake that sad task so we left it to his "family" to collect the remains of the little dog.

You might recall that I had to have my Labrador, Jason, put down all those years ago so I really do know how Fergie's owners felt.

****

In another of our houses along the way I came across this little poem, which may help to ease the pain for anyone with a similar problem looming. There was no title so I have named it:

The Last Battle

If it be I grow frail and weak
And pain should wake me from my sleep.
Then you must do what must be done
For this last battle can't be won.

You will be sad, I understand.
Don't let your grief then stay your hand.
For this day more than all the rest
Your love and friendship stand the test.

We've had so many happy years
What is to come will hold no fears.
You'll not want me to suffer, so
When the time comes, please let me go.

I know in time you too will see
It is a kindness you do to me.
Although my tail its last has waved
From pain and suffering I've been saved.

Do not grieve that it should be you
Who has to decide this thing to do.
We've been so close, we two, these years
Don't let your heart hold any tears.

anon

****

Now as far as we know, none of "our" houses was
haunted. Although some of them, or at least parts of some
of them, date back for centuries. Many of the more
substantial properties started life as simple farm workers'
cottages. Two up, two down, maybe a cellar and an

194

outhouse or two. These modest, simple dwellings had been added to over the years until they looked nothing like the originals. Double- glazing had been added to some, central heating to most. Most retained their character, through sympathetic re-modelling, whilst others struggled to avoid looking like a hotchpotch of architectural styles through the ages.

Whilst we never saw any ghosts there were many strange noises along the way. I've already mentioned thunderstorms and lightning strikes. They were readily identifiable and, though alarming at the time, one could accept them for what they were and drop off to sleep after the clamour had passed by. There were other noises, which, however, were not so easily endured.

Picture yourself alone at night in a strange house, which you know is about five hundred years old. By strange I mean, of course, unfamiliar! It is located in a forest in the middle of nowhere with no human presence for miles around. You're sleeping in a bedroom in the oldest part of the house and the wind is rustling the bare tree branches just outside the open window. It is the type of house where creaking floorboards sound like the groaning of an old sailing ship's timbers when straining against the load of a full complement of sail in a stiff wind.

In case you are wondering, yes I have been at sea (literally), in such circumstances.

No errant late-night reveller could ever hope to climb the stairs in this house and creep into bed without waking his (or her) spouse!

I was on my own this particular night as Sue had gone off on her travels again, Aga demonstrating in North Yorkshire and I'd got all the other regular night time noises filtering in to my room through the open window. As with the sound of storms, the screech of an owl or the barking of a fox I came to accept these as part of the rural environment and albeit having my sleep pattern disturbed, could roll over and attempt to shut them out.

Not so with more unusual noises. I had just managed to reach the welcoming arms of Morpheus that night when I heard a loud grating noise. Rather like an old door swinging on its hinges or a rusty iron gate being opened under protest. Now this house had several of both of these, so I was instantly wide awake and wondering what to do next. The noise happened again and then at fairly regular but intermittent intervals.

I could not hear any sound from down below, the dogs were not barking and no floorboards were creaking. I figured that no one was likely to burst into my bedroom so I accepted that it must have been the strengthening wind blowing something around, perhaps attached to the exterior of the building. I never found out exactly what it was but I suspected it to be the huge weathervane perched precariously on one of the gable ends.

I had just about made it back to the Land of Nod when, suddenly, there was a whirring noise, a sucking sound and the gurgle of flowing water, followed by a clunk and then silence. I lay there waiting, then again gurgle, clunk. In the middle of the night it is amazing what goes through your mind. Then I remembered that it was only the submersible electric pump in the cellar doing its never-ending job of emptying the cellar of rainwater and the products of a small spring which flowed continuously into it.

Every minute or so the pump would burst into action, depositing its output into a drain by the front door. Bit disconcerting really. If you didn't know, you could be standing at the front door when all this happened and you might think that someone had just flushed the loo and the contents had arrived, with all appropriate noises, at your feet. The fact that the drain outside couldn't handle the quantity of water, which then overflowed past the front doorstep, didn't help the situation.

The owner had explained the system to us before he left and told us that he had had a new pump fitted recently that was so much quieter that its predecessor. All I can say is that I was glad that we'd never stayed there before, as it must have been horrendous. We had asked what happened if the pump failed. We never got a real answer but we did have the name of an electrician and a plumber for emergencies. Maybe we should have asked for life belts in the cellar!

You might recall the winter of 2000/2001 with the almost continuous rainfall and severe flooding in the south east of England. Some poor folk not too far from where we were had been flooded five times that year.

Well, it seemed like a good portion of that rain found its way into that cellar and the pump would burst into action all too frequently, seemingly right beneath my bedroom floor. Not enough to wake one up but sufficiently loud to startle if already awake and perhaps prevent further sleep in the early hours of the morning.

As it happened, honestly, we did have a power cut around noon one day. Not due to adverse weather, although it was still only February, but, apparently, someone had been too enthusiastic with a JCB and had cut through a cable in one of the nearby fields. The break affected four or five villages around us, and the forecast for re-connection went from three pm, to four and then six pm. We watched with interest as the water level in the cellar crept towards the stairs leading to the rest of the house. I say stairs but these were ancient stone steps, their treads worn by countless feet over the centuries. God only knows what went on in that cellar over the years and what had been stored down there.

Anyway, I can't really turn a drama into a crisis this time. It had just started to get dark and just as I had lit a couple of candles, the lights flickered a couple of times and then, almost reluctantly, came on. As the cellar pump burst into action the water level stopped at the top of the last step on the staircase out of the cellar and we did not have to man the buckets. I dread to think of the consequences of a prolonged power cut in that house.

Several days later I awoke with a start, at around four o'clock in the morning. What the heck is a start anyway? We rarely talk about waking without one, do we? I suppose startled comes in to the equation somewhere but, anyway, you'll know what I mean.

I think the reason I woke up was the silence. No noise whatsoever. No wind, no creaking but, most of all, no whirring and gurgling from the cellar pump. Amazing how we can be alerted by the absence of noise to which we have become accustomed. I searched my mind for the last time I had heard the pump and when I had last been down in the cellar. Hell, I thought. I had not heard the pump for at least twenty-four hours and I had not had any cause to go down to the cellar for at least two days.

My mind boggled. I could just picture the scene down there. The water could be at least a couple of feet deep, things floating everywhere, the central heating boiler about to explode. The water may even now be lapping at the sitting room door. Of course, I could not get back to sleep but I did wait until around six thirty before I plucked up the courage to investigate.

My fears were unfounded. The cellar was all but dry. As it had not rained for about ten days by this time, there was so little water now seeping into the cellar the pump had not been pressed into action. Scary, though!

They did tell me later that the hurricane of October1987 that had devastated much of south east England had caused a power cut which lasted for four days. The water in the cellar reached five feet deep before the electricity supply was restored. The main water supply to the house was also cut off but they had plenty!

****

Talking of the '87 hurricane reminds me of another couple of instances involving cars and garages. One of our house owners used to leave his expensive Jaguar car outside his garage with the garage door open in front of the car. We wondered about this and the explanation was that at nesting time swallows would take up residence and the garage was off-limits until the young birds had flown the nest. Another owner did exactly the same, only this time two BMWs were involved.

What has that got to do with the '87 hurricane, you may ask? Absolutely nothing, but I did exactly the same a good few years earlier with near disastrous consequences.

Sue had been to an "antique" furniture auction and had proudly returned with a huge Victorian wardrobe which required a good deal of TLC before we could get it into the house and site it upstairs in one of the spare bedrooms. Sue had paid the princely sum of £18 for this monstrosity and there was nowhere else to put it but the garage as a temporary home pending restoration.

Unfortunately, we had just bought a new car, not a Jaguar I hasten to add, but nevertheless worth a great deal more than our newly acquired two ton piece of furniture which now filled the garage. To compound the problem, we were just off on a two week trip to Spain. It was October 1987 and we lived in Biggin Hill, Kent. Due to lack of garage space, the car had to be left out on the drive.

The hurricane occurred on the Thursday night before the Sunday we were due to return to England and reports in the Spanish press showed pictures of the devastation in our part of the world. We dare not phone our neighbours and it was with much trepidation that we travelled back from Gatwick Airport amid scenes of destruction reminiscent of World War One pictures of stripped tree-trunks on the battlefield.

We drove through all this carnage, round fallen branches and whole trees and as we turned into our road and saw with horror that slates and ridge tiles were missing from roofs. Garage door had imploded and many windows had been broken. There were damaged trees everywhere.

We had visions of our car being wrecked at the expense of our garaged wardrobe.

There stood our car. Not a mark on it, save for a covering of salt blown in on the storm. We glanced at the garage roof and saw a roof slate-sized hole right in the centre of the roof. On entering the garage we saw that the wardrobe was also unscathed but the roof tile lay in pieces right in the spot where the car would have been! Who said that an ill wind, etc? Well, he (or she) was right!

****

I digress, again! Same house, the one with the cellar, different night. I got up to check the plumbing in the wee small hours (pun intended). All was still again, not a sound to be heard, but I suddenly became aware of an unmistakable snoring noise seemingly coming from one of the other bedrooms. It took me only a moment to remember that I was alone in the house! Now, I reckon I'm not easily scared but you have to admit that this was more than a little spooky. Old house, dead of night, I'm wide-awake; no one else around and there's steady snoring somewhere close by.

Heavy torch in hand, heart in mouth, I set forth to investigate. As I entered each bedroom the snoring grew fainter but did not disappear completely. On returning to the bathroom it became louder again. It dawned on me that the noise was coming from downstairs.

The bathroom I was using was directly over the kitchen so I made my way down the creaking stairs and the snoring stopped. By now the dogs were awake and I had no way of proving that it was one of them with a bad snoring habit. I never heard it during the day when they were asleep, or again at night, so I hope it was one of them! I never found out.

In yet another house we were puzzled one night to hear faint noises emanating from up near the ceiling in the corner of our bedroom. We tried in vain to identify and locate the sound, which sounded like a cross between that of trapped insects, water dripping on stone or arcing similar to a minor short-circuiting of electricity. Nothing was visible from inside so we accepted that it could not be that important and retired for the night. We had forgotten about it the next day and sure enough it was there again the following night.

The culprits – I think!

****

On checking the outside of the house the following morning we resolved the mystery. Bees were flying in a continuous stream in and out of a very small hole underneath the gutter and between the soffit and the wall. The noise we had been hearing was the beating of their wings as they scrabbled through an extremely small aperture to get into their hiding place. We had heard stories of beehives above ceilings causing honey to drip down and leak through into rooms below but we decided that this one was in the wall and would not cause such a problem. We therefore did nothing at the time but made sure that the owners were aware of it on their return.

Talking of noises, we were relaxing in one sitting room early one evening when we heard a scrabbling from the direction of a downstairs bedroom. I opened the door to investigate and to my surprise found a fully-grown squirrel running round the room, having entered through the partially opened top window. Now squirrels are normally timid creatures that would run a mile when approached but, like most animals, they can turn aggressive when cornered. Well, as we all know, even a small bedroom has a number of corners and I was not about to prove how sharp a squirrel's teeth are by attempting to catch it. Keeping a wary eye on the unwelcome visitor I skirted the room, opened all the windows fully and using an old coat managed to get the squirrel back outside where it belonged. The joys of country living!

On another occasion, in the same house, we were sitting in the garden, as you by now have gathered we often did, when we heard an increasingly loud humming sound and looked up to see a huge dark cloud coming towards the house and us. It approached us at roof top level and recognising it as a large swarm of bees we decided the best policy would be to remain still and let it pass by. Fortunately it did and it disappeared at treetop height round the back of the timber-clad house.

We could still hear a loud humming and later to our dismay we found that the bees had found a way in through the cladding and were intent on taking up residence. As this really was a large swarm and a relatively small house we could not ignore its presence and had to resort to calling the local council in an attempt to have it removed. The council advised that they no longer tackled pest control so it was back to the Yellow Pages and eventually we found a local beekeeper who agreed to come out and capture the swarm.

Of course, he could not tackle the job for a day or two so we had to be extremely careful not to aggravate the bees in the meantime. We could not let the dogs anywhere near them and had to keep all the windows closed until they had been taken away. We had no air conditioning, of course. Not many houses in Britain do. Furthermore, as it was during an unusually hot spell, even for July, it was not funny.

The beekeeper eventually arrived and we stood well back as, clad in all his gear, he used his expertise to entice the now smoke-pacified swarm into his container and off the property. We were never so glad to see the back of a few insects!

****

And then there were the wind chimes. Now don't get me wrong. I actually like wind chimes. I have even bought them as presents for people who own the type of property where they can be used without annoyance to all and sundry within ear-shot. In the right circumstances I would even have some of my own as long as I could turn them off at night!

There are people out there, however, who "fly" them regardless of the proximity of neighbours. Come to think of it, some of them may do it because of them! Many's the time I took wind chimes down during our stays, or tied the component parts together to prevent them chiming.

Anyway, some people we know sport them because of the growing popularity in Britain of the old Chinese belief in Feng Shui. Now, I expect there are several Chinese and a good few Westerners laughing all the way to the bank over the increasing popularity of Feng Shui. People spend considerable sums of money for consultations and on re-designing their homes or offices to accommodate their new found knowledge on harmonious living.

Now I don't wish to offend any of you who might follow this particular trend but we in England have been managing quite well for a couple of thousand years without

Feng Shui. Well, a good few hundred years anyway. I certainly don't see any need to move my front door or the toilet because some Chinese man thinks that all my good ying, or is it yang, will disappear down the loo. Perhaps I should take the mirror off the bedroom ceiling too. We are getting a bit old for that anyway. Just joking, of course, on both of the last two statements!

An acquaintance of ours still believes that one of his businesses failed some time ago because his office was not laid out in accordance with the Feng Shui culture. After that bad patch he re-organized his office and, I have to accept, his business did begin to flourish. I prefer to think that it was due more to better business practice and the receding recession (if there can be such a thing) which caused the upturn in his fortunes but we'll never know.

Many of our owners phoned us from time to time to check that things were all right with their houses and pets back home. There's nothing wrong with that, of course, and I've already mentioned it a few times in these pages.

One night the phone rang at one thirty in the morning. It was Mr Avis calling from Sydney, Australia. Well, not actually Mr Avis but one of his employees in the hire car business.

"Can I speak to Mr X," the caller said to Sue, who, of course had just been abruptly awakened.

Mr X (our owner) had left his glasses in the hire care he had just dropped off at Sydney Airport and he had put his home phone number on the hire car documentation. The Avis rep had obviously not realised that he had dialled the UK.

Sue advised the rep that Mr X was still in Oz and if he waited while she found her glasses downstairs, she would let him have a number in Australia where he could be contacted on the next leg of his itinerary.

The rep apologised profusely to Sue for waking her up.

"It's OK," she said, "I had to get up to answer the phone anyway."

We're still not sure whether the rep got the joke but he was most grateful and in closing the conversation said, as most Aussies do, "See you later!"

Sue said, "Oh no you won't."

Chapter Fourteen

To The Manor Borne!

Two formidable electrically operated wrought iron gates, supported by stone pillars either side and topped with statues of two large dogs guarding the entrance, greeted us as we approached one of our most interesting houses for our first visit. We had passed by this Manor House many times on our travels around and through the county in which it is situated and we had always wondered who lived there and what the house might be like inside.

Set well back from the road, we had previously only glimpsed the three-storey, timber-framed structure with its multi-gabled roof, leaded windows and fascinating tall, crooked chimneys. As we had driven past many times at night we had seen that it was floodlit and tall shadows had danced across its walls as nearby trees, shrubs and bushes moved with the wind. We could see that it must have oodles of character and now we would have the chance to explore the house and grounds and learn some of its history. There were rumours that it was haunted so we were looking forward to an interesting time, if a little daunting in prospect.

As we drove down the long winding gravel drive we were shadowed by two majestic white swans gliding along one of the two lakes, which lay either side of the drive. They gathered speed as if to take off, reached V1 but abandoned lift-off before V2, (someone will explain the terms to you if you aeronautically challenged) and "crashed" to a halt in showers of spray just before the lake ran out.

Sweeping willow trees brushed the surface of the water and ducks in abundance moved reverently, but hastily, out of the swans' path. We thought it a little strange that the swans were so reactive to visitors - but more of that later.

We knew that the owners had a large black Labrador, still a puppy, but we were not prepared for the pony sized dog that came bounding up to us as we pulled to a halt at the end of the drive. Looking immensely fierce but falling over itself to be friendly, we were soon licked into submission and the dog boisterously followed us up to the front porch. A huge oak door nestled comfortably within the porch as though it had been there for hundreds of years, as indeed we later learned it had, and it swung open at our knock to reveal a stone flagged, oak panelled hall with a handsome chandelier hanging on a chain from the ceiling three storeys above.

Our hostess led us to the kitchen where she offered us coffee, prepared, we noted with relief, on the seemingly ubiquitous Aga in this part of the world and advised us that in addition to Austin, the Labrador, there were two Burmese cats in residence, Albert and Victoria.

We went through our normal briefing on all aspects of the house, where everything was and emergency telephone numbers; that sort of thing but two topics in particular were a little out of the ordinary. Firstly, Anne-Marie our owner warned us to be a little wary of the swans! Of course, we had to feed them but we had to be careful how we did it, as one of the swans in particular was very aggressive and would attack people without provocation. Brilliant, we thought but at least there was nylon netting all round their lake and their wings had been clipped – hence the aborted take-offs as we arrived. Secondly, we were advised that the house was reputed to be haunted so we shouldn't worry about any strange noises we heard in the night. Wonderful! We began to wonder if we'd made the right decision to accept this place as one of "our" houses. Anne-Marie explained that the last owners had been so troubled by the "ghost" that they had left after only a very short occupation. We were, however, assured that any supernatural presence in the house must be benign as the present family and the animals felt quite at home and, although strange sounds had been experienced and unexplained happenings had occurred, everyone felt quite at home and they were all completely relaxed about the whole thing.

Albert and Victoria

At this point I should perhaps try to describe the house in a little more detail. It dated as far back as the sixteenth century and in its earliest incarnation had been about three times as big. Reportedly connected by a tunnel to a nearby castle, it had previously had a huge cellar system although there is not one in evidence today. A large portion of the house burned down many years ago and the present structure came into being around the 1940s.

Large timbers formed the frame of the house and were striking on both the outside and interior surfaces. There was much oak panelling in most of the rooms, the inevitable genuine beamed ceilings and incredibly sloping floors in both of the upper storeys. Huge log fire- places featured in the main drawing room and dining room and another, only slightly smaller, fire-place formed the focal point in a cosier sitting room the family used on a day-to-day basis.

Uncountable mementos of foreign travel and antiques in abundance graced every room and the whole place was a delightful combination of elegance, comfort and atmosphere and, dare I say it, chaotic clutter! We thought that to occupy a house such as this, even for a short while would far outweigh the possibility of being attacked by swans and spooky nights.

If you need a better description of the house try and get hold of a copy of the video of the 1950s film "The Collector" starring Terrence Stamp and Samantha Eggar. We had both seen the film many years before and recalled that The Collector had abducted and then imprisoned a beautiful girl in the cellar of an old house. Well, this was the house. At least, the exterior and some of the interior was used but the cellar was fictitious and undoubtedly that bit was in some studio or other. Our owners possessed the video so we scared ourselves again during our stay and reminded us of the horrific (for those days) story. It was pretty exotic (or is it erotic) though, thinking that Samantha Eggar had used the very bath that we used during our stay.

Quickly, back to the script!

We did enjoy that stay and many others in the Manor House until the owners moved overseas and rented it whilst they were away. Many strange things did happen during our time there, the most notable being the following.

On leaving us in control one time our owners advised us that there had been a rat problem, however, the plumber had sorted it out! Rat droppings had been seen under our bath whilst some plumbing repairs had been underway and the plumber had recommended a particularly effective poison to put down. This had duly been purchased, laid down and nothing had been seen or heard since then, a week or so before we were due to take up residence.

All was well for a while until we heard noises coming from the cupboard under the stairs. I should add at this point that this cupboard was sufficiently large to house a refrigerator, a large chest freezer, a wine rack, all the cleaning materials and a vegetable rack. We were continuously in and out of the cupboard to access the necessities for a sensible diet, my cold beer and our white and red wine, not to mention the food. The house was full of noises anyway, particularly when it was windy, so we didn't think too much about it.

Just in case the rats had returned, I got some of the remaining poison recommended by the plumber and placed it behind the fridge. We then had to make sure that the dog and cats didn't get into the cupboard and waited for the noises to stop. We hoped that this poison was the type that rats took away from the house before they expired! At the rear of the cupboard there was a large hole in the wall leading to Lord knows where. Attempts had been made to block it up with an old eiderdown but it was pretty obviously the point of access for our unwelcome four-legged visitor.

One evening, not too soon after, Sue opened the door, switched on the light and there, about eighteen inches from her face was an enormous rat sitting on the vegetable rack tucking into some potatoes. I heard the scream about six rooms away and, although Sue is not normally fazed by creepy crawlies, mice and suchlike, she had difficulty saying the word rat. It came out (the word, that is) in a sort of high- pitched shriek and I was left in no doubt about the size, shape, colour and its proximity to Sue's face! Obviously the plumber's poison had not worked and the rat was thriving on it. There was less rat poison in the cupboard than the quantity I had put down so we could only assume that it must have been ineffective.

There was nothing for it but to call in the professionals. We didn't tell our owners but telephoned the pest control company whose number was listed on a board in the study and were promised a visit the following day. The rat man duly appeared with two large traps that he placed alongside the outside walls of the house assuring us that rats run along the walls and that these traps were very effective. Each trap was primed with a more powerful poison and we sought assurance that the traps were cat and dog proof before letting the rat man go. In the under stairs cupboard he placed some vicious looking poison blocks linked together on a big wire ring. We threw out all the fruit and vegetables, even the many oranges, which did not appear to have been gnawed at all.

In the days following we continued to hear scratching and scraping noises from the cupboard. The poison became more and more chewed. We still had to gain access to the fridge, freezer and wine stored in there, so each visit was made with much rattling of the door and a thorough inspection of the cupboard floor for droppings before entering. We also had to ensure that the door was shut behind us to prevent any rats entering the house.

The cleaner wouldn't even go near the cupboard! I had to fetch out the cleaning materials on her arrival and put them back when she left. The rat man came back, the traps remained empty and he topped up the poison in the cupboard.

After a few days the noises stopped and we thought that that would be the end of the saga. Then, we noticed the smell! Pretty innocuous at first and we didn't pay too much attention to it thinking it might be the drains. But it became worse, and we eventually came to the only conclusion possible. Considering the point in the house where the smell was strongest, it had to be the hall.

I knew I had to search for a body. A torch, fire-tongs, rubber gloves and plastic bags were the essential tools I needed as well as a strong stomach to face the task ahead. Initially, I had hoped that the beast might be far enough into the structure of the house that the odour would reach a peak, then subside but it hadn't and I could put the grisly search off no longer.

It's at times like these when you wonder whether house sitting is really what we should be doing in our retirement but I guess you have to take the rough with the smooth. You have to recall the idyllic dinners on the lawn by the lake, sipping a decent wine and eating a barbequed medium-rare rib-eye steak while the sun slips silently below the western horizon.

Dinner for Two, Al Fresco

Difficult to do as you probe around the deepest recesses in the cupboard under the stairs with the most obnoxious smell all around and wondering exactly what you are going to find.

Sure enough, I moved the fridge and there lay a big fat and very dead rat. Not quite at the maggoty stage, but not far off.

I do hope you are not reading this over breakfast!

It was only a moment's work and I had the body tied securely in a bag. Just to be on the safe side I decided that I had better look for more bodies and was pretty glad that I did. It was only when I moved the fridge further away from the wall, having looked everywhere else in the cupboard that I noticed what looked like some shredded paper in the back of the fridge. It was a nest. Pretty smart place to build a nest really as there was a constant supply of water from the drips of condensation from the cooling system and plenty of warmth from the fridge's electrics.

I removed seven bodies from the nest, all young rats, presumably killed by their mother's milk laced with the poison. I was much relieved that they had not developed into fully-grown rats. They would have taken over the whole house.

Once the rats, and the nest, had been buried deep in the garden and the cupboard had been thoroughly cleaned we got back to our normal routine in the household.

Our owners were mortified when they telephoned us to see how things were. We didn't intend to tell them until they returned but it sort of slipped out in conversation. They felt really bad about us having to put up with that kind of problem but then we'd have had to solve it ourselves anyway if it had been our house. They calmed down a little when the people they were staying with told them that they had had a similar problem not so long ago. One of the joys of living out in the country!

The rat man told us an interesting tale, which might be of interest to other "tradesmen" or anyone visiting other people's houses on business, or pleasure for that matter. One of his acquaintances had been doing some work, joinery I believe, at a large country house and was taken aback when, on his third visit, the police were there to greet him and he was promptly arrested.

He was charged with the theft of about £5,000 worth of jewellery from the house and led away, protesting his innocence. It was only some time later that the police found out the whole thing was an insurance scam perpetrated by the owner. She had sold her jewellery and then claimed it was stolen, hoping to be reimbursed by her insurance company. The poor tradesman never received as much as an apology from the police despite the slight on his character and his treatment at the police station, which included a compulsory, not so comfortable, bed and breakfast stay.

****

All the internal doors in the Manor were made of old vertical planking, good solid stuff, strong as they come and most fitting in that type of house. The latches were also made of wood, operated on one side by a lever and on the other, by a leather thong and toggle, a bit like old-fashioned bootlaces. The leather was threaded through the door to work the lever on the other side. They were primitive, though effective but a word of warning to any other people having the same type of latches.

You can easily get locked in or out on the toggle side of the door! We did, on more than one occasion. The first was when the thong broke on our bedroom door. We could not get in. All our efforts failed using knives, pieces of plastic etc prised between the door and the frame. It was only the fact that I had left one of the small bedroom windows open that saved the day.

We had no long ladders on the property but found a rickety old stepladder in a barn and used this to get on to a sloping bay window roof from which my fingertips could just reach the upstairs top window. Of course, it was bucketing down with rain. It always is on occasions such as this, in addition, dusk was approaching and I didn't want to tackle this job in the dark. Gingerly, I hauled myself up on to the sill and at full stretch managed to undo the catch on one of the main windows. From there it was relatively easy to clamber in and release that door catch from the inside, once I had negotiated all the pictures and ornaments on the window-sill.

Sue's mother, visiting us, as was her frequent wont, also got locked out of the bedroom but there was sufficient room between the door and the frame to use a knife to lever the catch up from the outside. The leather also broke on a dining room door but as there was another door to the room that was no problem to overcome.

The moral of this little tale is, if you have this type of door catch don't wait for the leather to break. Replace it on a routine basis. But then, if you do have them, you'll already know that won't you?

Then there were the swans. Inevitably, they escaped from their nylon netted lake and despite all our efforts to pen them in again they were strong enough to batter down the fencing each time we did. Now this would not ordinarily have been a problem. But one of the swans in particular was the most aggressive creature I have ever seen. Feeding time was a real problem. Fred (the male swan) would see us coming out of the house and would head for the lean-to where all the feed was stored.

It was then a real task to get down to the lake with the pellets without being attacked by him, aided and abetted by Freda (the female – we think). And I mean - attacked. A blow from an adult swan's wing can break your leg! I never actually had to run away but that was probably because I was always armed with a broom handle or garden spade. Not to take offensive action, I hasten to add, but there was many a time I warded off blows by means of one of these implements.

Even getting out of the car was a problem. We sometimes resorted to getting out of the opposite side door if the swans were about. Fortunately they were a little wary of Austin, the Lab, so walking down the drive with the dog was not a problem but wariness was the watchword when venturing down the drive alone.

Fred and Austin

Between each floor, the great oak staircase turned two right- angled corners and there was a half-landing of some size. A huge window sill, cluttered with ornaments, lovely leaded windows, as they all were throughout the house, and a lovely long-case clock adorned the lower half-landing. The clock wasn't in working order or, at least, wasn't ticking but the long door had an uncanny habit of opening at odd times. We were sure it wasn't vibrations from our footfalls on climbing or descending the stairs as it happened sometimes when everyone was either up, or down stairs.

It is difficult to describe the feeling, but try to imagine yourself on a dark night in a spooky old house. You are standing on the landing just about to come down the stairs. The flickering wall lights cast shadows everywhere and the house is groaning in the wind. As you look down to the half-landing, the clock door swings slowly open!

We never fathomed out what caused it to happen but we wedged the door shut to prevent it happening again.

Regrettably though, we never saw any ghosts. However, there were plenty of strange noises. At night the cats had the run of the house and our bedroom was on the middle floor. Many a time we heard footsteps above us, seemingly much too heavy for a cat and then there were the shrieks. I suppose we've all heard the strange noises cats can come up with late at night particularly if they are outside and other cats are invading their territory. More like a baby screaming, than a noise a cat should make. Well, during our times in the house we heard plenty of strange noises. We assured ourselves that it was the cats, or the wind or some other tangible thing, as we all know that there are no such things as ghosts.

Or are there?

****

Perhaps the strangest thing that happened to us in the Manor House, or anywhere else for that matter, was the case of the bending chandelier. You'll remember it being in the hall, hanging some thirty feet or more on a chain suspended about nine or ten feet from the floor. It consisted of a cast iron wheel-like structure with about ten U shaped brass tubes attached to the wheel supporting bulb holders. It hadn't been long fitted when we started going to the house and it was, still is, a most striking feature of the hall and you couldn't fail to notice it on entering or leaving by the front door.

I was at our Rottweiler house about four miles away on one of our disliked, but sometimes inescapable, overlaps and Sue was commuting to my house in the evenings for dinner.

She returned to the Manor, unlocked both front door locks, entered and neutralized the burglar alarm. At once she noticed something odd about the chandelier. One of the U shaped bulb holders was now L shaped and the bulb holder was horizontal instead of in a vertical position. Strange, she thought but assumed that Alison, the cleaner who had been there that day, or her husband who was doing some work in the garden, must have tried to change a bulb, slipped and grabbed the holder which had bent under his, or her, weight.

Sue didn't think too much about it that night but asked Alison the next morning what had happened. This was a "three day a week cleaner" house so that should give you another indication of its size. Alison told Sue that she had not been anywhere near the chandelier! Now, Anne-Marie, our owner was the type of person that would not mind what you broke as long as she was made aware of it, as most of our owners were, so Sue knew that there was no reason for Alison not to be telling the truth.

I came over to the house later that day and had a good look at things. I stood on a chair took hold of the lighting tube and tested the amount of strength require to straighten it, reckoning I could tell from that how much force had been required to bend it. With some effort I thought that I could have straightened it but I am well aware from dabbling in metalwork some years ago that it is so easy to kink, or break, a hollow tube without using the right tools, or fillers etc. So I left it as it was and we came to the conclusion that if it hadn't been bent by someone grabbing the tube to save themselves from falling off a chair or ladder then someone, or something, else had done it!

We left for home before the owners returned, as we often do to beat the traffic, and we had forgotten to leave word about this incident in our notes.

Sue was therefore not surprised the next day, when Anne-Marie telephoned to thank us and asked if anything untoward had happened while they were away.

Sue said straight away, "Do you mean the chandelier?"

Immediately she had said it Sue thought, "Oh God, that sounds as though I'm guilty!"

She of course then explained the whole story.

Some weeks later we were down that way again and called in to see Anne-Marie. The chandelier was still bent – only more so! We also learned that Anne-Marie and Alison had both been standing in the hall on one occasion and had seen the tube bending right in front of them.

A tall story, I know but it remains unexplained to this day.

****

The telephone call came in at nine thirty seven pm. The metallic, monotone computerised voice advised Sue that the river had burst its banks and, being on the flood plain, it droned, "Your property is in danger of flooding and should be evacuated without delay!"

My phone rang, at the rotty house, a few minutes later. It was Sue seeking my advice as to how she and her mother should escape the rising waters. A few hours earlier the lakes on either side of the drive had joined forces across it which Austin, the dog, thought was great fun but, without a four-wheel drive car, made the drive impassable. I had the 4WD with me so I could see myself having to carry out a night rescue for the potential flood victims.

Before doing so, we agreed that Sue should try to find a human voice instead of a computer recording. Finding the right person during working hours in our bureaucratic council system is bad enough, but late at night it was nigh on impossible. Eventually, after many re-routings and multiple-choice press-button options, Sue managed to find a person who actually knew what the real situation was. He was both very knowledgeable and re-assuring and advised her that the computerised warning she had received was the first stage in an automated system meant to advise residents that there was the potential for flooding, not necessarily that it was actually happening.

Those familiar with the differences between a tornado or hurricane watch, and warnings for the same, in the USA, will know what I mean.

Although by now the water across the drive was a few inches higher and the lake at the back of the house was seeking to join its friends at the front, as the house was a few feet higher than the surrounding land, Sue decided that they were better off staying put. She called me to let me know and, thankfully, I agreed that it was a good idea. After all, they couldn't really come to any harm in a three-storey house.

Just as a precaution, they moved what they could up on to the half landing although much of the furniture was too heavy to shift and, there was a lot of it! Satisfied that they had done all they could, making sure that their wellies were within easy reach and having made sure the dog and cats were out of harm's way, they went to bed.

It rained all that night and they didn't get much sleep but the phone didn't ring again and the water stayed out of the house.

All in a day, or night's work for the house sitter!

Chapter Fifteen

Under The Weather

The blizzard strengthened and became a white-out. We could now only see a few feet in front of the windscreen and we had no option but to stop the car. Although it was impossible to drive safely for any distance or speed, every few minutes I had to inch the vehicle forward to avoid the snow drifting against the side of the car and burying us. We were in great danger of being stranded on the highway, miles from anywhere in one of the worst winter storms to hit the mid-western United States in years.

Early on in these pages I mentioned that we had been stranded in our Devon cottage for a few days by snow and ice. There, we were safe and fully equipped with all we needed for a comfortable siege. It wouldn't really have mattered if it had taken a week. We had logs, candles, food, drink, heating and felt confident that all would work out all right – even with no electricity.

Here, it was different. We were on Interstate 70 just east of Denver, Colorado in the middle of a cold winter's storm and in deep trouble. More of that in a minute.

Except for our Colorado experience our only other brush with snow, which had caused us any problems was a winter house sit way up in the Yorkshire Moors. Archie, Sadie and Monty's people had sold their previous house and had moved temporarily to a shooting lodge of theirs whilst their "new" house was being renovated. Sue had agreed to look after the dogs and the house for them at the end of February one year, just before we were due to fly off to Florida.

As was becoming more and more usual, although we still tried to avoid it, we were apart as I was down in the south of England on "parental duty". However, it did coincide with an overlap in our house sitting commitments in the south so it worked out quite well. That is, until the weather up in Yorkshire took a turn for the worse.

Sue was supposed to finish on the first day of March, put the car in our garage at home, pick up a rental car on the second, drive down south and we were due to fly out to Florida on the third. The shooting- lodge owners were up in Scotland.

Sue and I kept in touch by e-mail and phone and we watched as a winter storm forecast turned into a reality as all roads in and out of Scotland became blocked. Sue reported that on her bleak moor the snow had reached ten inches and was drifting. She had awoken to a clear bright light and on opening the back door to let the dogs out she had been inundated by the snow piled up against the door! This was the morning of February twenty eighth, the wind was blowing and the snow looked set to fall and drift for the rest of the day.

Sue found a shovel and dug herself and the dogs out enough to get them into the drive. Looking around at this pristine, snow covered valley, now beginning to sparkle in the sunlight, she only wished she did not have to worry about getting off the moor to make the long journey south. At that moment, in the distance, she heard a vehicle obviously coming up the nearby lane. Lo and behold, at 8.30 in the morning just after the snow had stopped there was a tractor complete with snow plough, clearing the lane miles from anywhere!

The lane from the road below must have been at least a mile long and parts of it were around forty five degrees steep, its edge falling away to slopes just as steep down into the valley below. As there was a bed & breakfast place a little further up the lane (and I use the term loosely, lane, that is, not B&B) it was the responsibility of the local council to keep the lane open during all weathers. Sue strode through the drifts to the gate and hailing the driver, asked if he could plough the drive.

"Aye," he said, "if tha can get t' gate open!" (My Yorkshire's pretty good after all these years.)

Well, the gate was a five bar, field gate with three feet of snow piled up both sides. Sue set to work with the shovel, while the driver went on up to finish ploughing the lane. On his return the gate was open and he co-operated, largely helped by a five pound note, by ploughing all the way up the drive and also removing the snow from the whole area where our car was parked.

Monty in the snow

Fortunately, it did not snow again that day, or overnight, and Sue was able to get down off the moor with care, but with little trouble after the owners returned from Scotland. It could have been a lot worse, however, and she might easily have missed her flight. I would have been able to make it to the airport easily, having been in the south but whether I would have flown out to Florida on my own, we never discussed…..

****

Meanwhile, and several years before, back on Interstate 70 in the bleak flat plains of Colorado we were still in trouble. We had set out ten days before from St Louis to drive to Dillon, forty or so miles west of Denver. The Holiday Inn at Dillon was to be our base for a week of skiing at the resorts of Breckenridge, Copper Mountain and Keystone.

We'd had a great week despite our new car having refused to start as we tried to leave the slopes after our first day's skiing. We eventually had to get a tow truck to take the car down to Denver and relied on the hotel shuttle bus to get around for the rest of our stay. Although the car was only a few weeks old, the dealer had great trouble sourcing spare parts and we were not optimistic about getting it back to drive home. Eventually we telephoned the manufacturer in Detroit who, after much pressure from us, promised that the car would be ready – even if the dealer had to take the parts required from another car in his showroom!

We were so unimpressed with the service we received from the manufacturer and the dealer that on our return to St Louis we set out to replace our license plate with a suitable reminder of our experience. The state of Missouri had already issued LEMON so we had to settle for BAD-BUY which we installed on both the front and back of the car. During the rest of our three year stay we met many people who stopped and chatted to us about that plate and most sympathized with us when they heard our story.

The Chrysler dealer wouldn't bring the car back to up to Dillon so we had to take a Trailways bus down to Denver. If you could have seen us boarding the bus you would have thought we were moving house. As we had intended to do the whole journey by car we had everything with us, almost including the kitchen sink. Skis, boots, sleeping bags, food, wine, beer, winter clothes and everything else you might think of in preparation for close to a thousand mile journey across the mid-west in the middle of winter.

Anyway, we picked up the car in mid afternoon and decided to stay the night in Denver before setting out across the plains early the next morning.

We awoke to a fine, bright, but very cold winter's morning and managed to get out of Denver before the morning rush hour clogged the streets. We only had around nine hundred miles to go before reaching home. It was almost all on the same road, Interstate 70, so all we had to do was set cruise control, adjust the heating and listen to the music as we headed east across Colorado towards, Kansas and Missouri.

We had travelled about thirty miles out of Denver when it started to snow. The forecasters had said overnight and throughout the early morning newscasts that there would be snow flurries but there was no hint of a major storm brewing. However, before long the snow became heavier and heavier and the wind started to blow. The sky darkened and visibility worsened until we were just crawling along using the white line at the side of the slow lane as our guide.

Without warning a huge eighteen wheel truck came hurtling out of the gloom behind us sweeping past us only a few inches from our windows and disappeared up ahead. We were shaken to say the least and pulled on to the hard shoulder to sit out the storm. Every few minutes I'd move the car to keep us from getting snowed in. The radio cheerfully announced that Interstate 70 had been closed behind and ahead of us and the police were warning motorists to stay at home. Great, we thought, but at least we had warm clothes, sleeping bags and food and drink. We could ride out the weather and would not freeze.

As we wondered how long we might have to wait for conditions to improve we were amazed to see lights approaching us from ahead. It turned out to be a police car, all lights flashing, coming the wrong way down the highway. He stopped alongside us to see if we were OK and we assured him that we were doing all right, thank you very much. He asked if we would like to get off the highway and we jumped at the chance. We didn't want to risk any more of those truck drivers who must have had much better eyesight than us but, I suspect, a little less sense.

We turned the car around and followed the police car down the wrong side of the highway. He had to barge through deepening drifts to make a path for us and led us down an "up" ramp off the highway. We carefully followed his tracks along a country road and into a gateway leading to what looked like a small stadium. It turned out that this was a dog-racing track and some of the staff had managed to get in that morning before the snow had started. It was a Saturday morning and a race meeting had been planned for that day so the place was fully stocked for race goers who would never make it in.

Around thirty five people took refuge there that day and the staff, having contacted the owner, who never made it to the track either, looked after us so well. They opened the bar, cooked us lunch and dinner and let us use all the facilities. Most importantly, we had heat and shelter. Along with the people who were stranded, there were two horses and a number of dogs. The horses were found shelter in one of the barns around the track and the dogs had plenty of company in the stadium building to keep them happy. We all exchanged stories and developed what must be the relationships that only shipwreck survivors or castaways must experience. After a very pleasant evening drinking and yarning with our new found friends we retrieved our sleeping bags from the car and settled down for the night on the floor in one of the offices.

By next morning the snow had stopped and the whole landscape was bathed in bright sunshine. We showered in the owner's suite and breakfasted, courtesy again, of the racetrack staff. Some brave souls had already set out to test the roadways but we decided to await confirmation that the Interstate had been ploughed all the way east beyond the storm's reach.

Around nine o'clock we felt it was safe to venture forth to continue our journey. We said our farewells to our fellow refugees, promised to keep in touch with some of them which, of course, we never did, fired up the car and set off back the way we had come to get back on to the highway. The snow was around four feet deep at the side of the road.

On the Interstate only one lane had been ploughed and the surface was still covered with a layer of about two inches of frozen snow. We crawled eastward past many other cars and trucks which obviously had not had such good fortunes as ourselves. Many cars were in the ditch and a number of trucks had overturned. We wondered whether the truck that had just missed us on the highway the day before was one of these. I would not have been surprised, or even too dismayed.

On the news, we heard that hundreds of cars and trucks had been stranded by the storm over those twenty four hours. Many people had been forced to spend the night in their vehicles. Others had taken refuge in gas stations, farm buildings and weigh stations. We felt extremely lucky that we had stopped within striking distance of that racetrack just outside Byers, Colorado. We will be eternally grateful to the owner and we took steps to find out his name when we got back safely to St Louis. We never received a reply to our letter of thanks for his kindness and hospitality but if we are ever out that way again we'll call in and, at least, buy him a beer!

Chapter Sixteen

On The Moors

Unexpectedly, we returned in the summertime to the shooting- lodge high up in the Yorkshire Moors. We did two stints there that summer, as work on the restoration of the owners' farmhouse was taking far longer than expected. Damage to property in the area caused by heavy flooding the winter before was occupying local builders full-time, much to the frustration of people wanting less important work undertaken. We were delighted that it gave us an opportunity to live for a while in such a splendid spot although it was a round trip of one hundred miles for us to pick up our mail from home.

Mostly, when we were away, we either had our mail re-directed by the Post Office during long absences or we asked one of our neighbours to send the most important looking post on to us if we were away at several different locations. On this occasion, our neighbours were away too so we made the trip back home twice a week to keep things ticking over with the inevitable flow of correspondence with the outside world.

Driving north from Harrogate on the Great North Road we turned off eastward following the signs to Teesside. By passing Thirsk, the rising bulk of the North Yorkshire Moors National Park loomed on our right hand side and we took a further turn off to the right towards Stokesley. At Carlton-in-Cleveland we started our climb on to the moors. The gradient was advertised as twenty five per cent which, for the cartographically challenged, is a rise of one in four.

Pretty steep for any vehicle and that didn't take into account the hairpin bends with sheer drops below. Almost one thousand feet later we were rewarded with a magnificent view to the north and west encompassing the coast line to the River Tees to our north, to the shimmering outline of the Yorkshire Dales way over to the west. The weather was beautiful with bright sunshine, a clear deep blue sky and no heat haze. We could see for miles.

We crossed the moors for a while then we turned of the road on to the track which Sue's snow plough had grappled with a few months before. On the way we had passed over several disinfectant mats across the roads as this was the time of the Foot and Mouth Disease epidemic that had affected so many parts of England in the early months of the year. Signs were everywhere, warning that footpaths were closed and that motorists should not leave their cars when crossing the moors.

After a mile of "off-road" driving, traversing cattle grids and opening and shutting gates; there were six of them, we were welcomed as boisterously as ever by Archie, the old black Labrador, Sadie, the Gordon setter and Monty, the cross wolfhound/lurcher. We had not looked after any houses with such a spectacular view as this one. Sure, many others had glorious views but none of the others was on such a grand scale.

To the south the track wound its haphazard (and hazardous) way down the hillside to the road below and the valley stretched a good few miles before it turned a corner and wandered out of sight. To the north we looked up the valley to hills in the distance and our farmer neighbours at the end of the track another mile or so away. The lodge and its outbuildings were tucked into the west facing side of the valley. The steep slope of Bilsdale, covered in huge granite boulders and thousands of bilberry shrubs, rose another few hundred feet behind the house and dominated the eastern sky-line.

That left the western outlook. A mile across the valley, Reisdale sloped upwards and away from us dotted with pine trees, other woodland, ploughed fields, stone walls and craggy outcrops of rock. Swathes of late bluebells wafted in the breeze and contrasted sharply against the rich greens of grass and trees. Cattle and sheep were everywhere and only two other groups of buildings, both farms, could be seen as evidence that there were people, other than ourselves, in this beautiful part of the country.

High up on the Moors

Due to the Foot and Mouth outbreak we were not able to take the dogs for long walks across this spectacular countryside, but a short drive away, there was a sizeable area in which a café owner welcomed dog-owners to exercise their pets. A hundred or so acres of moorland had been fenced off and paths had been cut through the bracken and bilberries. There were a couple of ponds on the property, upon which several species of duck had made their homes. We used this facility and the café to good effect and both the dogs and ourselves welcomed the exercise, the fresh air and the views that our walks brought us. Regrettably, at fourteen years old, long walks were out of the question for Archie but Sadie and Monty much enjoyed their freedom.

We pondered much on the effects of Foot and Mouth on the rural communities, not just the farmers, but all concerned with the country way of life and the many offshoot businesses affected by the disease. Hotels, bed and breakfast places, pubs, cafes, tour operators, village shops – there were many more. Cattle markets, auctioneers and sheep-shearers to name but a few. In fact, we learned that a new form of livestock auction had been born because of the crisis. Video and internet auctions were taking place and many head of cattle changed hands by these unorthodox methods.

We sat and watched the livestock in the valley below knowing that only ten or so miles over the hills to the North West, livestock were being culled in an attempt to stem fresh outbreaks of this virulent disease. We dreaded the day when we might hear and see the awful process taking place on our (temporary) door-step. Our farmer neighbour had even told us that he had heard talk of another local farmer saying he was contemplating deliberate infection of his stock to obtain the somewhat generous compensation on offer from the government. Fortunately, our neighbour had informed the authorities of what he had heard, although what ensued we never found out.

Over the years the sheep roaming the moors had been "trained" to recognize their owner's territory; a process called hefting. We never really learned how these sheep knew not to stray beyond these imaginary boundaries, as there were no fences or walls to keep them penned in. Although it didn't happen in the area in which we were staying, one of the many casualties of Foot and Mouth was the hefted sheep phenomenon. In areas where whole flocks of sheep were taken off the moors and killed to prevent the spread of this dreadful disease it would take generations of new sheep to instil the flock with the awareness of their allotted grazing territory.

Our only recently met, farmer neighbour offered us some rabbits which we found difficulty in refusing. We accepted three. Now Sue is a pretty good cook as I might have already told you and she has, during her career, tried her hand at most things culinary. However, her many experiences had not included the gutting and skinning of rabbits! Those of you who are squeamish, please look away now!

I mentioned earlier Sue's participation in the operations on our cats in Saudi Arabia. Well, the cats were warm, cuddly and alive, they didn't smell and there was very little involved with the procedure in the way of messy stuff. However, with rabbits that had been hung for several days, too many probably, it was a completely different kettle of fish – so to speak. Smelly fish, at that! Nonetheless, we put on a brave face and some rubber gloves and armed with sharp knives and a cleaver we set to on the kitchen table. I managed to help with one of them before I had to get some fresh air.

Sue soldiered on and completed another before she also gave up. She did casserole them in the Aga but, as far as I know, they are still in the freezer as we didn't have the courage to eat them after our unpleasant experience with their preparation. The third hapless rabbit ended up as fox food outside on the moor!

It was kind of our neighbours to offer us the rabbits and they did offer more – which we politely declined. However, they were a welcome source of really good, large fresh eggs during our stays.

As you might have guessed, rabbits were in abundance all around us. I have never seen so many in one place. We even saw more black rabbits and it was difficult to avoid them on the roads, particularly at night.

Also present in great numbers were pheasant. Now, although we were in a shooting-lodge and up on the moors we never expected to see so many of these magnificent birds. From our windows we could see as many as thirty at a time and it was not really until these visits that I realised the wide range of different colours in the plumage of these birds. No two birds seemed exactly alike and their iridescent feathers ranged from yellows and oranges through red to blue, purple and black – plus a few shades of everything in between.

Spot the Pheasant!

One expects coloured plumage in tropical climes, or on birds of the jungle but this must be the most beautiful of the larger birds seen in numbers in the British Isles, albeit that they originated from India. An even larger population might be expected if shooting did not take place this year – another potential casualty of Foot and Mouth.

Another Day, Another Dog

Beautiful as the pheasant is to look at, I cannot say the same for the sound of its voice. There cannot be many other countryside sounds as harsh and raucous as the call of a fully-grown pheasant. The nearest comparison I can make is that of a high pitched old-fashioned car horn. You know the type I mean. A big brass horn with a round rubber bulb at one end which, when squeezed, gave out a horrible attention grabbing screech. Not that I ever used one of course, although my first ever car was old enough to have the little illuminated arm-type exterior traffic indicators.

Much gentler was the sound of the cuckoo. I have mentioned sighting this parasitic, rarely seen but often heard, bird before during one of our stays in East Sussex. Here on the moors, however, we had one in permanent residence nearby and its incessant cry became an "earsore" from dawn to dusk. As it was over mid-summer, the hours of daylight in these latitudes stretched from around three thirty in the morning until ten thirty at night. How the darn bird kept it up that long I'll never know.

I probably would not have mentioned the cuckoo again here but for its constant proximity and the fact that in the afternoons it often used to sit in a huge sycamore tree at the edge of the garden. Other birds would dive-bomb it, presumably to chase it away from their nesting area. Not so interesting in itself, as that sort of thing happens all the time in nature. What was amusing though, was that the cuckoo never seemed to stop its call all the way through these frequent attacks. However, when one of the attacking birds came too close or actually made contact its call would deviate from the standard almost musical cuckoo to a much higher pitched dual tone cuck - ooooh. The cuckoo was still around when we left so I guess it was well used to the aggression and would live another day to indulge in its annual despicable habit of brood parasitism.

There was no lack of water up here for the various animals and birds on the moor. Long disused jet and ironstone mines had left scars on the landscape, some of which had filled up with water from natural springs or drainage off the high moor. Bits of jet could still be found on the surface near the old workings.

Geese and ducks thrived on all the ponds except one close by. No weeds or other pond life lived there either. The pond had been formed by someone long ago damming a stream flowing down a steep gully and it was dark but clear, and deep. "Ryan", the local farmer neighbour told us that they had had the water tested some time ago and that its Ph content was such that it would not support life. Supposition was that it was something to do with the old mine workings but we found it strange that all the other bodies of water roundabout were teeming with life.

Whilst in the area we took the opportunity to revisit Sue's birthplace near Stockton-on-Tees. Although she had moved away from the area at a very early age she had been back a few times with her mother to visit family who had continued to live there. As with many villages, if you stripped away all the modern tat, plastic and chrome, modern houses, etc, you could still see what a pretty place it must have been more that half a century ago. That's progress, I guess.

One thing that had survived for nearly one hundred years was the "famous" transporter across the River Tees. Now, I had never heard of it until Sue told me about it some years before, but apparently it was one of the civil engineering wonders of the north of England in its day and, reportedly, unique in its construction. Certainly I had never crossed a major river on a platform hanging by cables slung under a huge gantry. Powered by electricity, a maximum of nine cars were sedately transported across the water from one side of the Tees to the other. An antiquity in these modern times but still used daily by local commuters.

Driving through and out of Middlesborough and into one of the old coal mining villages around its perimeter, we were again reminded and, as always, strange though it may sound, were surprised that areas of industrial ugliness and cramped living were only a few short miles from olde-world villages with charming timeless character and beautiful, unspoiled rolling countryside.

Our time on the moors came to an end and we left with some sadness for our next commitment looking after Tatti, the lively Golden retriever in East Sussex. We knew that our next spell with Archie, Sadie and Monty would be in their new house, which, although of great character and in a fine setting, could not match the splendour of the location of "our" shooting-lodge on the moor.

Chapter Seventeen

Bits And Pieces

We all know that Labradors like carrying things, sticks, shoes, underwear - those sorts of things. These lovable dogs will greet you on your return to the house, or when you come downstairs in the morning and joyfully bring you something as a token of their affection. It might be your best socks, new underwear or worse still, dirty underwear, or something from the dustbin. Not anything edible of course as it would have been devoured long before. In fact one of our clients summed up Labradors pretty well.

"They only have two things on their minds, food and sex."

He was not far wrong. Those of you that have not seen a healthy Labrador eat have not witnessed the ultimate eating machine. Having owned two male Labradors myself I can also vouch for the fact that they are pretty enthusiastic about the other aforementioned activity, given the chance.

All Labrador puppies seem to have been taught soon after birth that the most wonderful source of a quick snack is the dishwasher loaded with dirty crockery and cutlery. How they never managed to cut their tongues on sharp knives always amazed me. However, Labradors were not unique in their dishwasher licking skills. I mentioned poor old Fergie the Border terrier in a previous chapter. His party trick was to climb right inside the dishwasher to seek out the more tasty delicacies. Fortunately, we never closed the door on him!

Perhaps there is a third passion enjoyed by Labradors; water. Both Jason and Spey my own two labs would seek out the nearest source, whether it was a lake, river, stream or even a shallow dirty puddle. Usually, the muddier the better. Butch and Sundance revelled in the water. Retrievers and setters also fall into the water-loving category. One big Gordon setter we looked after had his own unique style where water was concerned.

My sister's place boasted a plake. Not quite big enough to be classified as a lake but certainly an oversized man-made pond and so it received the honour of the compromise; plake. Brad, the Gordon setter would run full speed towards the water, take off from the bank, soar through the air with all four legs splayed out and land right in the middle. Maybe that's not so unusual but he would then put his head right under the water as if searching for an imaginary stick on the bottom. Of course, the water was never clear enough for him to see anything but this did not deter him. On surfacing, his head would look remarkably like that of a seal, with his hair all slicked back around his ears.

Among the most unusual items brought to us by Labradors were hedgehogs. One lovely old black lab called Archie had a fondness for the spiky creatures and often, on his late night walk just before he was due to retire for the night, he would insist on bringing home a hedgehog. There is no sound stranger than a dog trying to bark with a mouthful of hedgehog. Painful too, I suspect. Archie's companion, Sadie, a large Gordon setter, would join in the fun and they would both career around the garden celebrating Archie's hunting achievement.

Archie's owner had warned us that this might happen and had advised us of the only safe way of extricating the hapless creature from his jaws. Without this specialist advice I would probably have tried the leather glove routine together with the tried and trusted biscuit diplomacy accompanied by the appropriate commands of leave, give, drop or the "in" command of the day. No! Our advised method was to get hold of a garden spade. Then we should make sure Archie could see the spade, raise it in the air and threaten to hit him with it!

The effect was startling and worked every time. Archie would drop the beast immediately and, as a bonus, the appropriate tool was readily to hand to pick up the hedgehog and restore it to freedom. Three nights running was the record for hedgehog hunting.

I hasten to add that Archie was never actually struck by his owner or by us. The mere threat of violence always did the trick. In addition, all the hedgehogs we freed this way (it might have been the same one every time) seemed no worse for the experience as they were (or it was) always gone when we checked where we had left them (or it) the night before!

Monty, Sadie & Archie

Hedgehogs weren't the only things Archie proudly brought to us. One fine summer's day we had all the doors and windows open and were surprised to see Archie approaching us, in the house, with a blackbird in his mouth. It was obvious that the poor bird was dead and, indeed, we later deduced that it had flown in the back door, along the lengthy hallway and had met its demise against the study window. Feathers and other deposits led us to this conclusion.

Remembering previous successes with hedgehog extraction I led Archie out into the garden in search of the spade. However, all attempts at the "garden spade" persuasion method of mouth-contents retrieval, which had been so successful with hedgehogs, failed dismally. By now Archie's two companions, Monty and Sadie had joined in the fun and there were feathers everywhere.

It was about this stage of the game that I had a fleeting glimpse in my mind of Archie's owner in Barbour and green wellies striding across the grouse moors with shotgun on one shoulder and spade over the other as part of his standard shooting gear. Yes, of course, Archie had been a working gun dog all his life and there must have been a tried and tested way of getting birds away from him.

In the end, it was easy. I just took hold of one of the bird's legs, gently held Archie by the scruff of his neck and uttered the magic word, "leave". Without any fuss he let go and the blackbird was given a decent burial.

We became used to spaniels bringing us ducks, pheasants and doves over the years but were not quite prepared for one spaniel turning up during one walk with a deer's "hind" leg. (No pun intended.) There wasn't much left of it save the hoof and bones but it was over three feet long and fairly fresh. By that I mean it wasn't yet smelly.

Having mentioned sneezing in an earlier chapter reminds me again of Monty, a lurcher-cross, acquired from the RSPCA by Archie's owners. They had visited the local branch to help their parents select a dog after the demise of both of their much-loved pets. Whilst there, as many people do, they fell in love with one of the "inmates". Monty just could not be ignored and they ended up taking him home "as a companion" for Archie and Sadie.

Now Monty was the most friendly, gentle dog one could wish for. He was as obedient as any boisterous eighteen-month old can be, that is, not very, but he did have a few unusual habits. When Sue or I sneezed, or blew our noses and in February's rain and gales this was not an unusual occurrence, Monty leapt to his feet, barked, jumped up and down and became very excited. His owners had warned us of this so it did not take us by surprise.

However, we were not forewarned about the clocks. On our Sunday morning ritual of clock winding, only three in this case, we were amazed to find that as soon as I had taken the first clock off the mantelpiece Monty showed an even more animated reaction and did not stop barking until I put the clock back where it belonged. Needless to say I did not let him into the hall whilst I wound the long case clock.

It would have been interesting to research Monty's pre RSPCA history. We did not believe he was mistreated but maybe his previous owners suffered incessantly from hay fever or colds and had Monty witnessed a burglary involving clocks? We'll never know.

****

There are other sources from which to obtain a dog but most discerning prospective dog owners select the breed of dog they want and then look for a good breeder. You just pop along to see what is on offer and make your choice of the puppies left in the litter. Not so! It doesn't always work quite like that.

We heard of one couple who had just bought a house in Clapham and were thinking of starting a family. They had decided that it would be a great idea to acquire a Labrador puppy for the new baby to grow up with. Off they went to a reputable breeder and were shown a delightful litter of newly born black Labrador puppies. Expecting to be able to select the puppy of their choice, to be collected later when it was ready to leave its mother, they were astounded to be subjected instead to an interrogation as to their suitability for ownership of their new charge.

"Clapham?" The breeder exclaimed after she had enquired where they lived.

"You do have a house, I hope?"

Now, maybe Clapham is full of flats or bed-sits. I don't really know. My only experience of that part of the world was the not very appealing view from grimy train windows as I passed through Clapham Junction in the days when I braved the discomfort of commuting into London on British Rail.

On being assured that they did actually own a house, the next question was, "I hope you have a garden?"

"Yes," they said, "but it is not very big."

"Well, what are you going to do about walking the dog? Labradors do need plenty of exercise you know."

By now, more than a little taken aback, our prospective purchasers said, weakly, "Well, we thought we'd take him for walks on Clapham Common, which is quite near to our house."

"Clapham Common," she shrieked, "you can't walk one of my dogs there. Nasty dogs walk on Clapham Common; you'll have to take him to Richmond."

Meekly, they agreed. However, their ordeal was not yet over. They were asked to come back a few weeks later.

"Is that when we can choose our puppy," they asked.

"Choose your puppy," the breeder again shrieked. "That's not how it works, at all."

Apparently it was a matter of finding out about the owners' character and habits, waiting to see how the individual puppies developed and then pairing them to each other.

It might seem a strange way of going about it but I can see a lot of sense in that selection procedure. No good matching a lively, energetic dog that might show a tendency to dominate others in the litter and to hunt for its food, to an elderly couple who merely wanted a companion in their home. Similarly, the farmer or active sportsman would not want the timid puppy that tended to lie around all day. Heaven only knows what a young family would need!

Having told that tale, it is a fact of life these days that even the RSPCA or any of the many other dog rescue centres will ask searching questions of prospective owners before releasing dogs into their care. Quite right too and the old adage of "a dog is not just for Christmas, but for life" still holds good. Too many dogs are still taken on by people not realising the extent, and the cost, of the commitment and the sometimes hard work required to keep dogs healthy and happy.

Talking of dog walking, I have mentioned, probably several times, how owning a dog can be rewarding in so many ways but there are dangers as indeed there are in any circumstances. Many accidents happen in the home when least expected. Falls, electric shock, cuts and burns, perhaps all to be expected as part of life's rich pattern. But dog walking? You might expect the odd sprained ankle or pulled muscle by too much exertion or after a slip on a muddy path.

One of "our" cleaning ladies told us the sad story of her husband who had a mishap when walking their own dog in fields not too far from their house. He climbed a stile over a hedge; put his foot on the tread on the downward side, which promptly and without warning, collapsed under his weight. There was a crack as he landed heavily on one leg and he fell in the mud. He suffered a compound fracture and the bone, sticking out of his leg, was covered in mud. In great pain it took him several hours to get home and a while longer to get to hospital to have his injury treated.

The end result was that his wound became so infected that he had to have his leg amputated! Never let it be said that dog walking is a completely safe occupation.

****

Devoted dog owners probably treat their dogs' litters much differently than breeders and with a lot more affection. We came across one lady who had three delightful King Charles Cavalier Spaniels. They were adored and it showed.

Some time before, one of them had had a litter of ten puppies and her owner was moved to write the following poem.

Ode to a Litter or Two!

Ten little Cavaliers eating round one plate.
Cal and Tony "trained" to Bedford, then there were eight.

Eight little Cavaliers causing havoc in the garden.
Carmen's gone to Belper, then there were seven.

Seven little Cavaliers up to some more tricks.
Ghilly's now in Pembury, then there were six.

Six little Cavaliers – would we have some more?
Mel and Lulu went to Staplehurst, then there were four.

Four little Cavaliers chewing Mave's sweet pea.
Oscar travelled to Blue Bell Hill, then there were three.

Three little Cavaliers thought they'd nowhere to go.
Cindy left for Wimbledom, then there were two.

Two little Cavaliers, our work is nearly done.
Amy's gone to Croydon, then there was one.

One little Cavalier, Jasper all alone.
When his mistress gets back from holiday, to Hever he'll
be gone.

Charming. This was also the lady who telephoned twice from a hotel in New Zealand in her first six days away just to see if her spaniels were doing OK with us. Of course, they were. So were the two cats and the prize-winning sweet peas in cold frames she had left in our charge one February. However, it was our first time there so I could understand her apprehension. We learned later that the sweet peas under cold frames during our stay had indeed won first prize at the local flower show later in the year.

Not surprising as there were max-min thermometers in each cold frame and we had to keep the frame lids in exactly the right position to maintain an even temperature. Just the right amount of moisture had to be applied during our five week stay and various thicknesses of covering had to be applied dependent on the predicted nightly temperatures. More than once we were out in the middle of the night to make sure the beloved peas were OK. The sweet peas required more attention than the dogs!

You might remember me mentioning our two spaniels, Fisky and Lucy, earlier on. They were both "unwanted" dogs before we took them on and we were glad that we were able to give them a new lease of life – even though both of them had to be passed on to members of our family due to my journeys abroad with my employment.

Another prospective rescued dog owner was quizzed in depth by the staff when he turned up at Battersea Dogs Home to look for a Labrador to replace one that had died a short while before.

"We'll need to come out to see that your house and garden are suitable for a large dog, sir," a member of the management said.

"Fine," responded the visitor and gave his address.

"Castle Howard, North Yorkshire," Mr Howard said.

Now, I'm not quite sure whether they ever sent an inspector out but, for those out there who may not know of Castle Howard, we are talking here of one of England's finest country houses surrounded by hundreds of acres of beautiful grounds and park land. Needless to say, the new dog settled in to a great new life after its spell in the dog house!

Getting back to the subject of dogs' reactions to human behaviour I must mention again the two flat coat retrievers who featured in my earlier tale about keeping me awake and joining in the "fun" when the house I was in was struck by lightning.

Often I took a guitar with me on our travels and I usually made a good deal of noise practicing, taking advantage of the lack of close neighbours in most of our houses. Something I could not do back home in Harrogate. The two flat coats would not even let me strum a few chords without joining in with full voice. They would immediately put their heads back and yowl in accompaniment. I would not have minded too much but they were never in tune! The only way I could play and sing was to isolate myself at one end of the house with the dogs at the other, or in the garden. Their owner also owned a guitar so goodness knows how he ever managed to pick up his instrument and play without taking similar precautions.

I later discovered that Monty, the lurcher, reacted even more violently than the flat coats to my guitar. I'm pretty sure it wasn't my playing. At least I hope it wasn't!

Back to Labradors. I am sure that all Labrador owners, or other dog owners for that matter, have had instances where their pets have eaten something they shouldn't. Remember Fisky and the chocolate at the beginning of the book? I would not have believed that a dog could eat so much chocolate at one "sitting".

How many times have you left a choice piece of steak, or similar tasty morsel, too close to the edge of the kitchen work surface, left the room for an instance and hey presto, steak gone? Have you ever left hors d'oeuvres or biscuits on the coffee table and turned your back for a moment? The bigger the dog the higher the risk, so to speak!

We did have a small Border terrier that knocked a tray containing two glasses of wine and some Pringles off a coffee table one evening. The wine went all over the light-coloured carpet and one of the glasses broke. By the time we entered the room after hearing the crash the Pringles had been demolished and we were so glad that the owners were still in the house, having not yet completed their briefing before setting off on their travels.

We've never really had any dramatic disasters with dogs breaking things or eating food other than their own. I guess the worst was when my mother-in-law lovingly made the Christmas cake one winter and brought it down to my sister's where we were all to have Christmas dinner that year. It was left at the back of the kitchen work-top for a while, just long enough for Emma the chocolate lab to sniff it out, get it on the floor and devour more than half of it.

What could we do? It was two days before Christmas and the cake was over half gone. In fact, it was irreparable and we knew that Sue's mother would not be best pleased at what had happened.

Eventually we came up with the idea that, as the cake had looked so tantalising, we had not been able to resist trying it out early and had succumbed to the temptation by eating all of it. We therefore ate about half of what was left, gave the remaining piece to my parents and swore them to secrecy. In fact my mother said it was so nice that, "could she have the recipe?"

We never knew whether the story had been "swallowed" but the matter was never mentioned again and many cakes have been received from the same welcome source since then.

Another Labrador, nameless this time, but real nevertheless, and living near Orpington in Kent, had an awful reputation as a wanderer. Awful as in full of awe of course, not in the other sense. He lived down wind of a sausage factory that acted like a magnet for him. He even had to cross the railway line to get there and would often return with notes attached saying where he had been and what food he had been given. A local butcher would also regularly telephone his owners, as the dog would not leave the shop at closing time.

The local fish and chip shop was another of his favourite destinations and we have it on good authority that he sometimes preferred fish and chips to his regular sausage and meat scraps diet. Eventually, he became so used to the journey, over a mile away, that he would get on the local bus by himself and hitch a ride to the chippy and back. Fortunately, we never had to look after this wandering lab and fortunately again none of our charges have ever left home while we have been in residence with them.

****

Small dogs had their moments too. During our time in Devon a friend of Sue's who lived in the north of Scotland asked her to buy a "genuine" Jack Russell and to ship it up to her. As you might know, Jack Russells originated in Swimbridge, Devon and in fact, there's a pub there of that name to prove it. The Reverend John Russell apparently had a passion for hunting and breeding hunting dogs in addition to his ecclesiastical duties and he bought his first terrier, Trump, from a milkman in Oxford. Exactly when the breed was established is not clear but almost certainly it was between the years 1795 and 1803, during John Russell's life span, or soon after. The breed was developed from the fox terrier for its tenacious character and ability to go to ground after rabbits and foxes.

Sue subsequently bought the dog, a bitch in fact, and by a circuitous route involving several airline friends we shipped it by air (I never really understood how one could ship something by air) via Bristol and Glasgow to Inverness. The dog arrived safely and settled in to its life at Boat of Garten near Aviemore in the highlands. We did not see it again until it had been bred and had had a puppy, which had grown to the same size as its mother by the time we arrived for a visit.

Mother and puppy were doing fine but did not get on together at all. Fights were common, particularly around feeding time and it was not advised to try to separate them during disagreements. Fingers were at risk. Terriers are notorious for biting, and mother and daughter had been known to unite and attack anyone who came between them. We therefore tried not to get involved in any contretemps during our stay. One evening at dinner, ours, not the dogs', there was the inevitable scrabble under the table which quickly developed into a full-scale war. Ankles were in imminent danger and things were becoming serious.

Without blinking an eyelid Sue's friend surveyed the situation, bent down and picked up the top dog by the scruff of its neck. I use the words top dog accurately as the underdog came up off the floor too, firmly gripped in the jaws of her daughter, or mother, I couldn't tell which. As if it were a regular occurrence and I suspect it was, Sue's friend calmly walked to the back door, dogs still attached to each other, and threw them out into the snow. The meal resumed as if nothing untoward had happened and later the dogs meekly came back inside, all aggression having disappeared.

As far as we know they lived "happily" ever after.

Touching as much wood as I can find, we have never had a break-in at any of the houses, which have been in our charge. One night, however, we were disturbed by a knock at the door and a perfect stranger (well, she looked almost perfect to me) was standing there, obviously in a state of distress. She was looking after her parents' house just up the road and had returned home late in the evening to find the burglar alarm activated and sounds of movement in the darkened house. Understandably, she was frightened and was looking for assistance.

Having established that the police had been called I set out with a torch and a suitably large stick to see if I could help. The night was pitch black. There were no lights along this country lane and there was no moon. Their house was up the lane a little way, set back from the road and was in complete darkness.

As I approached the house, the security lights came on and I decided that, before entering, I would circle the building to look for signs of forced entry. There were no windows broken and no signs of any of the doors having been forced. I took a firm grip on my stick and slowly pushed open the front door. There was a noise from inside the sitting room. I had no clue where the light switches were.

Was I being silly and should I leave this to the police? Something told me that there was a simple explanation to all this. The security lights had not been on, there were no signs of forced entry. Surely it must be an inside job.

Gingerly I opened the sitting room door, found the switch and flooded the room with light, taking care to stay just outside the door flattened against the wall. Well, you only have to have watched Miami Vice once and you soon know all the right moves. I took a swift look around the door frame. The room was a mess, ornaments broken, pictures askew and papers everywhere. I stood in the doorway assessing my next move. Without warning, I sensed an object coming straight at me and with lightning reflexes I quickly moved outside and just managed to shut the door in time.

I had almost taken a fully-grown crow directly in the face.

Relieved, I passed on the good news to those outside and set about releasing the intruder. From the mess in the fireplace it was obvious that the chimney had been the point of entry. All the windows were locked, of course, and looked like they had not been opened for years. We eventually found the keys, opened the windows, turned off all the lights and after a while the frightened bird found an exit and flew off into the night. A close call, but all in a day's work and just another aspect of the house sitter's repertoire.

****

Annette, a friend of ours had been asked to look after another friend's huge retriever called Happy and had just returned home with the dog, having been to a very good party. Her parking space in the lane behind her house meant that she had to park with the driver's door parallel and very close to her Yorkshire dry-stone garden wall. It was well after midnight, the dog was desperate to go to the loo and as she started to open the door Annette put her foot on the lane outside. Happy forgot about ladies first, tried to jump over Annette and in the process the hand brake was released. The car rolled an inch or two forward, as automatics tend to do, and trapped Annette's leg in the car door as the door was now wedged firmly against the wall.

As the car was parked on a slight down gradient there was no way to move it either "manually," i.e. with her foot, or using the engine. Both occupants by now were desperate to get out but Annette could not reach over to open the passenger door, at least to let the dog out. She even thought about pushing Happy out through the sunroof but could not reach that either. Happy had not yet learned that he could squeeze through small openings at this stage in his life.

So, it was now well after midnight. Annette and Happy were trapped in the car with no way out. She wanted to avoid getting anyone else involved at that time of night especially because it had been a very good party. But time was passing, the car was creaking and the pressure on her leg was increasing. There was only one thing for it – sound the horn to attract attention to her plight.

This she did, whereupon lights came on in neighbouring houses. Curtains twitched, faces appeared and eventually help arrived in the shape of a very old man. He tried in vain to push the car, Annette was shouting at him. They eventually managed to let Happy out but Annette's leg was still stuck fast, the car could not be moved so there was nothing else for it but to call the emergency services. Not exactly what Annette wanted at all, having had more than one or two beverages not too many hours before!

Eventually, both the police and the fire brigade arrived. Annette was in real distress by this time and a helpful policeman asked her if she was all right. She did what any, quick thinking sensible girl would do under the circumstances. She burst into tears and said she could do with a stiff brandy. She even told the policeman where in the house the decanter was and he brought a generous glass to her, which she promptly drank. Meanwhile, several burly firemen had manhandled the car away from the wall and she was at last set free. The, by now, substantial crowd eventually dispersed, many thank-yous were expressed and Annette and Happy retired to the safety of her house after their ordeal. The police and firemen politely refused the grateful offer of a drink!

On another occasion Annette had been pleaded with at very short notice, again, to look after Happy. That was fine but she had accepted the offer of a trip that very day on another friend's rather up-market brand new yacht. She felt that she could not leave Happy at home for the whole day so she set off with him in her car to meet her friend at a hotel. Annette went into the hotel to meet her friend, leaving Happy in the car with a window slightly open. When she returned to her car Happy was nowhere to be seen. She couldn't understand how Happy could have escaped from the car. She had only left the window open a few inches!

Someone told her they had seen the dog disappearing through a hedge at the bottom of the car park and, after much searching, she found him in a stinking muddy canal and had great difficulty in catching him and getting him back into her car. Trouble is, the plan was to leave her car there and it was her friend's car in which they were to travel to the yacht mooring. Although some superficial drying and cleaning was attempted, Happy immediately transposed the friend's car seats from their original pristine condition to a sort of wet, muddy hairy morass.

On arrival at the mooring Annette let the dog out, to do what dogs must, gave it some water and then left her friends car window partly open for ventilation but with less of an opening than previously before boarding the boat.

They had slipped the mooring and were some way into the river when to Annette's horror she saw Happy frantically claw his way out of the very small gap between the car window and the roof, jump headlong into the river and start swimming furiously after the boat. He was obviously determined to join the party. All the others on board were gazing forward, oblivious to the presence of their frantic follower.

The dog was not going to make it so Annette asked her friend to stop the boat and after reluctantly coming about, they picked up the big, wet, muddy dog. If you have ever tried to pick up a large, wet retriever you'll know it's not easy. To hoist one up and over the side of a boat from a river is nearly impossible and, of course, what does a dog do immediately it gets out of the water? Yes, free showers for all in range. Mud and water was sprayed generously over all on aboard and on the hitherto gleaming vessel.

There is no finer test of true friendship than to dirty his, or her, car and new boat on the same day. We still don't know whether that friendship is intact but we do know that Happy was. Happy, that is.

Not long after that one of Annette's friends asked her if Happy would oblige in mating with her own black Labrador bitch. Annette agreed, on Happy's behalf, but all efforts to get the dogs to take an interest in each other came to nothing. The ladies eventually decided that there was only one thing for it. What would humans do to increase their chances of success? They would have a quiet, special dinner with candles, romantic atmosphere, all that stuff. So Annette and her friend decided to go out for the evening leaving the dogs alone with bowls of special food.

The lights were dimmed, romantic music was heaped on the stereo and candles were lit. They tiptoed out the door and returned a few hours later. The food was gone, the music was still playing and the candles had all but expired. As for the dogs, they were fast asleep at opposite ends of the room and there was no evidence at all of a romantic interlude having taken place. However, something must have happened that night as several weeks later four puppies arrived, two Labradors, one black and one golden together with a pair of retrievers, one black and one gold.

Annette had been an air stewardess for many years and she had related many amusing and interesting stories to us about her experiences.

One such story that involved animals was about a colleague of hers, we had better call him Bill, who arrived at his hotel in New York after a transatlantic flight. He unpacked his bag in his room and took a relaxing shower. On emerging from the shower he was amazed to see a cat strolling around looking very much at home.

Thinking it must have come in when he entered the room, he took a closer look and was surprised to see that it looked very much like his own cat that he had left back home in England earlier that morning. The cat sidled up to him and with a gradual feeling of horror Bill realised that it was his cat! It dawned on him that the cat had crept into his bag after he had finished packing before the flight and that it had slept all the way over the ocean, through immigration and customs and the trip to the hotel.

The airline was very understanding and allowed the cat to fly back with Bill to the United Kingdom but he could not ignore the strict quarantine laws. Regrettably therefore the cat had to spend the next six months in quarantine as a penance for his unauthorised transatlantic jaunt.

****

Having said that we have looked after dogs, cats, cattle, ponies, swans, ducks, sheep, fish and chickens (have I forgotten anything?) there has never actually been an occasion when we have bitten off more that we can chew, so to speak. There was, however, one instance where it nearly happened.

We had been recommended to a couple in the wilds of the Yorkshire Dales who lived on a small farm with their seven (yes, seven) large dogs, two cats, three horses, goats, some cattle and a large number of Merino sheep. We went to dinner with them one night together with the people who had recommended us and had a delightful evening in their old farmhouse, complete with a venerable Aga.

However, the dogs were almost uncontrollable and the goats were prone to attacking their reflections in our car. We were therefore more than a little relieved that we never received a call from them for our services and believe that the couple rarely left the property together for more that just a few hours.

Chapter Eighteen

Nothing Is Forever

For over ten years we looked after dogs and other people's houses, most of which were in the south of England, mainly in Kent and East Sussex. We didn't mind the travelling as it brought the chance to regularly visit my elderly parents on the coast at Bexhill and my sister near Hartfield also in East Sussex.

Our time was our own to spend how we wished and we enjoyed the differences in all the houses we took care of and the disparate characters and nature of the various dogs and other animals in our charge. We had so much fun and enjoyment over the years. Each time we visited one of our houses things had changed a little. It could be a different time of year, the garden might have been modified, or the house, or both. A much-loved pet may have passed on or a new puppy or kitten may have arrived.

We could not have thought of a better way to combine our love of animals with travelling, a varied life-style, keeping fit, playing new golf courses and being able to maintain close contact with my family.

However, time marched relentlessly on and many of our favourite dogs were falling by the wayside as the years went by. Fortunately for us, none actually died while we were in residence but there were several occasions when we drove away with tears in our eyes knowing that the next time we came their way they might not be around.

I mentioned a few of "our" dogs to which we had become most attached over the years in my dedication at the beginning of this book.

I had lost Jason all those many years ago but I clearly remember the grief I felt then and could readily identify with the losses our various owners felt when their "best friends" left them, and we shared their feelings of loss. It was somehow vastly different going back to houses where a favourite dog was no longer in residence. There were always others to take their place - but you'll know what I mean about that "empty space" if you have ever lost a dog that you loved.

Sadly the passing years did not ignore my family either. First my mother, then a few years later my father succumbed to failing health and we said farewell to them with heavy hearts. They were eighty eight and ninety years old respectively when they died so they had had a pretty good innings which helped to soften the blow somewhat. However, my sister Raine at only fifty six years old was diagnosed with cancer and after a lengthy, valiant fight left us only three short months after my father.

We still have not come to terms with that great family loss. Raine was so healthy and full of life it did just not seem right that she was taken so early in life with so much left to do and enjoy.

The day before she died I said to her. "If you see mum and dad along the way, please give them my love."

She said she would, and I then said to her, "I'll see you some time in the future."

She looked up at me from her bed in the Royal Marsden Hospital, smiled at me and said, "'Bye Trevor, I love you. OK, yes I hope to see you again - but don't make it too soon."

It's at times like that one feels so helpless and it certainly brings home the fact that, really, nothing is forever.

Lucy, Raine & Emma on Ashdown Forest

Raine's ashes are now buried only a stone's throw from the "enchanted place" high up on Ashdown Forest of Winnie the Pooh fame that I mentioned earlier in these pages. It's the place she loved most and where she, and we, had spent many happy hours walking our various dogs over the years. It seemed the right spot for Raine to end her foreshortened journey through life.

It was after these tragic events we realised that our trips to the south were no longer quite so important and we started to wind down our visits until we finally cut our ties with our last remaining "clients" in the southern counties. You'll remember that it was Raine who had inadvertently started us off in our dog sitting adventures. It was now time to hang up our leads.

We look back on our long years of dog sitting with much nostalgia and absolutely no regrets. We made a lot of good friends. We met some nice people too!

There's that well-known saying about a dog being man's best friend. Those who have had dogs will know just how true that can be. Treat them well, be firm, give them lots of TLC and they'll be your friends for the whole of their lifetime. Those that have never owned a dog just don't know what they're missing.

****

Whether we will we ever have a dog of our own again remains to be seen. Maybe not, and I don't think we could put up with a puppy at our stage of life, but you never know.

Arnie, one of our favourites

There might just be another Jason or Arnie look-alike out there somewhere who needs a good home.......

Printed in the United Kingdom
by Lightning Source UK Ltd.
117731UKS00001B/4-21